I Do Not Like Thee, Dr Fell

All in Fav

I Do Not Like Thee, Dr Fell

&

All in Favour Said No!

Bernard Farrell

MERCIER PRESS

IRISH AMERICAN BOOK COMPANY (IABC)
Boulder, Colorado

MERCIER PRESS
PO Box 5, 5 French Church Street, Cork
16 Hume Street, Dublin 2

Trade enquiries to CMD DISTRIBUTION,
55a Spruce Avenue, Stillorgan Industrial Park, Blackrock, Dublin

Published in the US and Canada by the
IRISH AMERICAN BOOK COMPANY
6309 Monarch Park Place, Niwot, Colorado, 80503
Tel: (303) 652 2710, (800) 452-7115
Fax: (303) 652 2689, (800) 401-9705

This book is published with the financial assistance of The Arts Council, An
Chomhairle Ealaíon, Ireland.

The Arts Council
An Chomhairle Ealaíon

Printed in Ireland by Colour Books Ltd.

CONTENTS

PREFACE

I Do Not Like Thee, Doctor Fell was my first play and, as such, was written with the greatest of ease. I was not working to deadlines, nobody was stopping me in the street to ask what was it about, I had no anxieties about either audiences or critics – all I wanted to do was to please myself.

The year was 1977 and I was having a ball. Nobody (outside my immediate family) knew of my theatrical aspirations. I was single, free, more than slightly irresponsible, interested only in football and dances, holidays and films and, further along, in my work as a clerk with Sealink.

When I finished the play – in my own good time – I first thought that I'd send it nowhere. I felt that nobody, except me, would ever like it or its peculiar humour. Then some of my family read it, thought it funny, and I began to think that maybe some amateur group might risk a production. Eventually, in a moment of glorious hilarity, I decided to start at the top and to send it to The Abbey Theatre.

Some months later, the Abbey's new Artistic Director, Joe Dowling, wrote to me. He asked if I would like to come in and meet their script editor, the playwright Tom Kilroy.

I did – and I was so overcome that I continually called him 'Mr Kilroy' despite his quiet insistence that I call him 'Tom'. In between name-games and corrections, he told me that Joe Dowling had read the play and had loved it, that they all found it very exciting – and that it was Joe's intention to premier it in the smaller Peacock Theatre in March.

He did – with Paul Brennan directing a wonderful cast that included a young Liam Neeson. The reviews were dream-reviews, the audience flocked to see it, it transferred (twice) to the main Abbey stage and went on tour – all in 1979.

I was now firmly 'outed' and my undercover literary activities were at an end. The following year, when Joe Dowling told me that my second play, *Canaries*, would be the Abbey's presentation in the Dublin Theatre Festival, I immediately resigned from Sealink. Against the advice of many sensible people, I had now allowed my hobby to become my life.

7

My third play for the Abbey was, everybody said, based on my office days: my experience of strikes, union/management squabbles, stabbings-in-the-back and the luckless square-pegs working in round-holes. And it was hard to deny that *All in Favour* did come from my days behind a desk – but I would insist that its characters were drawn from the terraces of football grounds as much as from factory floors and executive suites.

It opened in April 1981 and enjoyed a wonderful run and a later revival for the Abbey's summer season. And the following year, it had its American premier at the South Coast Repertory Theatre in California ... the same month as *Dr Fell* began its American tour.

Already these two Abbey plays were partners and I had a choice of being with one or the other. It was the sunshine that took me to Los Angeles.

All In Favour opened the company's theatrical season and, as such, was launched with a Hollywood-style Gala. Fireworks, stretch-limousines, celebrities – all combined to take my breath away ... and maybe even turn my head. But perhaps it was my upbringing or my Irishness that told me that all of this was just icing – and that, back home, there were new cakes to bake.

Now, fifteen plays later, these two plays still remain very special. *Dr Fell* I thank for starting me out and *All In Favour* I will always regard as a loving memory of a life I left behind.

With this new publication of both plays, may many re-live the moments of excitement as when I first saw them – and, yes, may they laugh (as I did and still secretly do) with relief and recognition.

BERNARD FARRELL

I DO NOT LIKE THEE, DR FELL

I Do Not Like Thee, Dr Fell was first presented at the Peacock Theatre, Dublin, on 15 March 1979 with the following cast:

PADDY	John Molloy
JOE	Garrett Keogh
SUZY	Billie Morton
ROGER	Liam Neeson
PETER	Tom Hickey
MAUREEN	Eileen Colgan
RITA	Kathleen Barrington

DIRECTOR	Paul Brennan
DESIGNER	Frank Conway
LIGHTING	Tony Wakefield

FOR MY PARENTS

ACT ONE

Scene One

A large, bare, third-storey room where the encounter group will meet. No furniture or trappings except for cushions scattered about and a tin bucket in the corner. Entrance door at left. Door to off-stage Contemplation Room at right. Window at back is bricked up. A locked box, containing a telephone with a lead-in wire, is fixed to the wall beside the entrance door.

It is evening – about 8.00p.m. Paddy – an old man in dungarees – is carefully sweeping the floor, quietly singing 'High Noon' to himself. Hold for ten seconds. Joe speculatively enters. He is about 25 – a nervous type, he carefully carries a travelling bag. He watches Paddy for a while. When he speaks, he stammers.

JOE:	Ex ... Excuse me.
	(Paddy continues sweeping and singing, unnoticing)
JOE:	I be ... beg your pardon.
PADDY:	Ah, good evening, sir – you're number one.
JOE:	Nu ... Number one?
PADDY:	Yeah, number one – the first to arrive. *(Pauses)* You are here for the group thing-a-ma-gig, aren't you? The head shrinkers?
JOE:	Miss Bernstein's Group Therapy Se ... Session?
PADDY:	The very one – I call them the head shrinkers. Are you here for that?
JOE:	Yes.
PADDY:	Well, find somewhere to sit, sunshine – they'll all be here in a minute. *(Joe moves around. Paddy sweeps)*
JOE:	Are ... are you here for Therapy as well?
PADDY:	Me? Are you joking or something? Would I be sweeping up this kip if I was one of them? *(Mock officialdom)* I'm what's known as the Group Attendant – that's what I am. The Group Attendant.
JOE:	Oh I see.
PADDY:	Not my real job, of course. I'm really the caretaker of this whole building but, on a Saturday night, I become the Group Attendant. Do you get me?

11

JOE:	Yes. *(Takes out cigarettes)* Smoke?
PADDY:	What's that?
JOE:	Wo ... would you like a ci ... ci ... cig ...
PADDY:	Cigarette? No, never touch them, sunshine – bad for the 'oul bronchial tubes, you know. But thanks all the same.
JOE:	Is it all right if I ...?
PADDY:	Oh, fire ahead sunshine, fire ahead. Just watch the ash.
JOE:	Oh yes.
PADDY:	*(Placing the bucket)* Here, you can use that.
JOE:	Oh thanks. *(Paddy sweeps)*
PADDY:	What's the trouble anyway, sunshine? The nerves? The gargle? Women?
JOE:	No, no I'm just inter ... inter ... inter ... I've just got reas ... reas ... reasons ...
PADDY:	Reasons? Yeah, I understand. Well, I only hope they fix you up all right.
JOE:	What are they like?
PADDY:	What's that, sunshine?
JOE:	I ... I ... was wo ... wondering what are they like.
PADDY:	What are they like? *(Laughs)* Ah, they're usually all right.
JOE:	Are they?
PADDY:	Yeah, they're all right ... I suppose.
JOE:	*(Quietly)* Just all right?
PADDY:	*(Looking carefully at Joe)* Well, truthfully now, sunshine, I'll tell you what they're like, in my experience: they're not a bit like you – that's what they're like. Not your type, if you understand.
JOE:	No? Wh ... what's their type?
PADDY:	I shouldn't be saying this but, in my opinion, Weirdos – that's the type. Give you an example – last week they had a fellow who thought he was Henry the Eighth. Seriously, really thought he was Henry the Eight. Dirty 'oul bugger. A good boot in the arse is what he needed.
JOE:	*(Laughing)* Go away!
PADDY:	That's all he needed – a good runnin' boot in the arse.
JOE:	So wh ... what did they do for him?
PADDY:	Ah now, there I leave you, sunshine. What they did for him is no concern of mine. I'm just the Group Attendant, you understand – I lock them in here, I go home, look at the telly, talk to the missus, read the paper, see how the

	nags went, put the chiselers to bed (if I can find them), come back here, bring in the grub, go home, have a kip, come back in the morning and turn them all loose. And what happens in the meantime is no concern of mine.
JOE:	Oh, I see.
PADDY:	And I still say you don't look the type. Truthfully, now, if I saw you outside, I'd be surprised to see you coming in here. I'm surprised to see you *in* here now.
JOE:	Well, I was just cur ... cur ... curi ...
PADDY:	Curious?
JOE:	Yes, Curious.
PADDY:	Killed the cat, didn't it? Curiosity. Isn't that what they say? Curiosity killed the cat.
JOE:	Yes.
PADDY:	Ah, don't mind me, sunshine – I'm only talking. You'll be all right. You'll see ...
	(A sudden commotion outside. Suzy Bernstein rushes in, carrying an attaché case and clip-board. In her twenties, she speaks with an American accent, is alert – all action and efficiency. She is followed by Roger – in his twenties, exudes good breeding, is politely enthusiastic)
SUZY:	Goddam cabs – Jesus no – taxis! I'll never get used to your expressions.
ROGER:	*(Laughing patronisingly)* The Great Divide, you know – the little difference. *Vive les petites differences.*
SUZY:	Right on, Roger. Evening Paddy.
PADDY:	Good evening, Miss Bernstein. Just one arrived so far.
SUZY:	Two. This is Roger – a comely nomad I encountered on the stairs. *(Checks clip-board)* Now, you are ... ?
JOE:	Jo ... Jo ... Joe Fell.
Suzy:	One name only – we all start equal. Right Joe, say hello to Roger – relax, relate, communicate. Blood brothers in embryo.
ROGER:	Hello, did you say your name was Fell?
Suzy:	First names only, folks – it's a rule. *(Checks clip)*
ROGER:	Ah, but a simple *lapsus lingua* – slip of the tongue – from Joe. You did say Fell?
JOE:	Joe Fell.
ROGER:	Fell, Fell, Yes, Doctor Fell – that's it. Are you familiar with Martial?

JOE:	Who?
ROGER:	Martial – the Spanish writer. First century.
JOE:	No, I ... don't think so.
ROGER:	With your name, you must know his 'Epigrammata'?
JOE:	No.
ROGER:	You don't know his *Non amo te, sabidi, nec possum dicere quare?*
JOE:	*(Puzzled)* No.
ROGER:	Well, you should. Or at least the celebrated translation by Thomas Browne (1663–1704) – what was it now? Oh yes – 'I do not like thee, Dr Fell/and why it is, I cannot tell/I only know and know so well/I do not like thee, Dr Fell'. You've heard that before, surely?
JOE:	No ... I ... I don't think so.
ROGER:	Oh, well it's quite well known.
Suzy:	*(Writing on clip-board)* Joe and Roger, okay, We have one, two, three to come. A Peter, a Rita and a Maureen – beautiful Irish names. Everything A-OK, Paddy?
PADDY:	Yes, Miss Bernstein – the soap and towels are inside and I've set the table ...
Suzy:	Fine, we'll just check that out. *(Leaves for other room with Paddy)* Don't run away, kids ... be right back.
	(Short uncomfortable silence)
ROGER:	Very efficient woman that.
JOE:	Do ... do you know her?
ROGER:	Oh no no no no, just my considered – very considered – opinion.
JOE:	Oh.
ROGER:	Opinion is the medium between knowledge and ignorance – do you agree?
JOE:	What? Oh yes.
ROGER:	*(Thoughtfully)* Oh yes, ignorance and knowledge ... *(Silence)*
JOE:	She's an American, isn't she?
ROGER:	*Mirabile, mirabile,* Herr Dr Fell – she is indeed. From Texaleto in Utah.
JOE:	Utah? Arizona.
ROGER:	Pardon me?
JOE:	Texaleto is in Ar ... Arizona.
ROGER:	Arizona? No – Texaleto, Utah. The lady clearly said so.

14

JOE: I re ... read in a book by Zane Gray that Texaleto was in Ar ... Arizona.

ROGER: Zane who?

JOE: Gray.

ROGER: Gray? Gray? No.

JOE: He writes cowboy books.

ROGER: Ha! No, Texaleto in the state of Utah – no doubt about it. She said so.

(Silence)

JOE: Is this your first Th ... Therapy here?

ROGER: All life is a Therapy, Joe – but yes, this will be my first with Miss Bernstein.

JOE: You've been to others?

ROGER: Oh, yes, the odyssey of self-discovery is a perpetual search: Berlin – very efficient, London – prissy, one in Rome – too emotional, Oslo was really excellent.

JOE: Yeah?

ROGER: Touch therapy there. The flesh contact – a true discovery. Man to man, soul to soul, mind to mind ... beautiful, beautiful ... Apollos, Davids, Titans ... bodies *homo antiqua virtute ac fide* ... virtue and loyalty ...

JOE: Is that where they all take off their clothes?

ROGER: *(Loftily)* Yes, you could put it like that, I suppose.

JOE: I don't think they do that here.

ROGER: You've been here before, then?

JOE: No.

ROGER: Well then, how can you possibly assume ...?

(Peter and Maureen enter. They are in their thirties – a suburban couple. Maureen carries a suitcase.)

PETER: Hello there – the Suzy Bernstein Therapy Group?

ROGER: *(Full of new enthusiasm)* Yes, yes, *entrez, entrez*, abandon hope and all that ... face thy doom ye slaves of Rome ...

PETER: Ah good – come along, love. Mind the step. Good girl.

MAUREEN: Oooh, a nice big room, isn't it?

ROGER: I'm Roger, this is Joe – you must be Peter and, shall I guess, Rita?

PETER: I'm Peter all right – this is Maureen, my wife. Who's Rita?

ROGER: I've no idea really.

MAUREEN: *(Looking around)* The window is all blocked up. *(Laughs)*

15

PETER: Then why did you say Rita?

ROGER: Well it had to be a Rita or a Maureen.

MAUREEN: *(Hearing her name)* Yes?

PETER: Why did it have be a Rita or a Maureen?

ROGER: Ah, the initial confusion of souls in search. My apologies
– Miss Bernstein read out the names of those to come
and there was a Rita and a Maureen. So I speculated that
your wife was Rita.

PETER: No, she's Maureen.

ROGER: Quite – my speculation was incorrect. Rita is the *persona
in absentia.*

PETER: She's the what?

ROGER: The missing one – the one to come.

PETER: Ah, I see – and that's how you knew I was Peter.

MAUREEN: No chairs though. Funny.

ROGER: Exactly. And I'm Roger and this is Joe. *(These shake hands,
muttering greetings)*

PETER: Maureen, say hello to Roger and Joe here. Come on now.

MAUREEN: How are you Roger.

ROGER: I'm very well, Maureen – not Rita, eh? *(Shakes hands)*

MAUREEN: No, Maureen.

JOE: Hello.

MAUREEN: Hello Joe. *(Memorising names)* Roger and Joe.
(Suzy rushes in again, followed by Paddy)

SUZY: ... and dinner at 23 hundred hours on the dot and don't
forget the phone check ... oh, hi there, people – Peter and
... Rita?

ROGER/PETER: *Maureen!*

SUZY: You win a few and you lose a few – nice to see you. I'm
Suzy, your Group Co-Ordinator for tonight, Okay? Right,
just settle down, people – get acquainted while we wait
for ... eh ... Rita. Relax, relate, communicate.

PETER: Will we put our suitcases in the other room ... ?

SUZY: Oh yeah, Jesus yeah. Suitcases. Now folks, suitcases,
overnight bags, watches, clocks and all that stuff remain
outside. Paddy'll put them in a closet just outside the
door. All you need is a toilet bag – toothpaste and such-
like. We divest ourselves of everything here – first our
holdalls then our hang-ups. Get it?

ROGER: *(Holding aloft a single toothbrush)* Voila.

16

SUZY: Ah-ha, been down this road before, eh Roger? Okay others, take what you need and give the rest to Paddy.
(Maureen rummages in the suitcase)

JOE: *(Weakly)* Is there a gentlem ... gentlem ... gentlemen's ...?

SUZY: A which, Joe?

JOE: A jacks where I can ...

ROGER: I think he means the loo.

SUZY: Oh yeah, sorry Joe. Folks, the washroom, the kitchen and
the Contemplation Room are all out here, okay? Great.
(Checks clip-board again) Going to have a really good session here tonight.

PETER: *(Watching Maureen)* Are they there, Maureen?

MAUREEN: Yes, I have them. *(Takes out a small toilet-bag)*

PADDY: *(To Maureen)* I'll take that case, love.

MAUREEN: Oh, thank you very much. *(Struggles with clips)* It's rusty.

JOE: *(Going off into room)* I just want to get some stuff out of
my bag.

PADDY: Fair enough, sunshine – I'll get yours later.
(To Maureen) That's grand, love. *(Leaves)*

ROGER: Splendid weather today, Peter.

PETER: For the time of year, Roger.

ROGER: You like the sun, I can see. Nice tan. All over?

PETER: Ah, I don't bother too much – got most of that on the
building site. I like the summer though. *(Quietly)* Women,
you know.

ROGER: Pardon?

PETER: You know, women – flashes all over the place – frilly
dresses, cheese-cloth, transparent ... oh-ho, it all happens
in the summer. Randy weather.

ROGER: Oh yes.

PETER: Good for a bit of yabadaba-doooooo.

ROGER: *(Coldly)* Yes, quite.

PETER: Never mention that to the wife, though. A quiet flash is
what you want. Nothing like the sly flash ...

ROGER: My summer is the body. The heat. Therapeutic.

PETER: Thera-what?

ROGER: You know – good for the metabolism.

MAUREEN: *(To Peter)* He's nice – he called me love. Twice.

PETER: Who did?

MAUREEN: The man with the bags.

17

PETER:	*(Looking after Paddy)* Did he? *(To Suzy)* Who's that man Miss Bernstein?
SUZY:	Suzy, please. That's Paddy – The Group Attendant. Joe? Are you okay? Find it all right?
JOE:	*(Arriving back)* Yes. I'm fin ... fin ... I'm grand.
SUZY:	Good. Paddy? One more bag here. *(Checking names again)* Got to get this show on the road fast. Paddy'll take that bag, Joe. Okay people, take a look in here, familiar- ise yourselves while we wait for ... eh ... Rita. Paddy! One bag here. Paddy! Paddy!
	(Suzy, Roger, Maureen and Peter leave for Contemplation Room, Joe waits)
PADDY:	*(Running in)* Jaysus, such shouting – she'll have me as bad as the rest of you. Oh, no offence, sunshine – how's it going so far?
JOE:	Oh grand.
PADDY:	Any sign of Henry the Eighth?
JOE:	No – wh ... where are you putting my bag?
PADDY:	*(Laughs)* What have you got in it? A bomb? Or just a few sticks of gelignite? Do I hear it ticking?
JOE:	No ... it's ju ... just that I got a loan of that ba ... bag and I do ... don't want to lo ... lose ...
PADDY:	Ah don't worry about it, sunshine – I'm putting it in the closet out here. It'll be safe and sound. You'll be locked up in here, the bags will be waiting out there and I'll be watching the telly at home. Gas set-up, isn't it?
JOE:	Do you know where Tex ... Tex ... Texaleto is?
PADDY:	A pub, is it?
JOE:	No, a place.
PADDY:	Texaleto? No, where is it?
JOE:	It's in Arizona.
PADDY:	Go way.
JOE:	Yes. Wonder what happens here next.
PADDY:	*(Sternly)* Ah, a few orgies – roaring and screaming – run- ning around naked ...
JOE:	Do you think so?
PADDY:	I'm only codding you, sunshine. Truthfully, I haven't a clue and I care less. I see nothing, I hear nothing (because the whole kip is sound-proof) and I ask no questions – and that suits me.

	(Rita cautiously enters. She is 50/60. Carries a handbag)
RITA:	Hello.
PADDY:	*(To Joe)* Jaysus, Queen Victoria. *(To Rita)* Yes madam?
RITA:	My name is Rita. Is this the Suzy Bernstein Group Therapy Session?
PADDY:	Indeed it is, madam – come in. Do you have a suitcase?
RITA:	A suitcase?
PADDY:	A suitcase.
RITA:	No, just my handbag ... But you may take my coat.
PADDY:	That's grand, madam. Make yourself at home – Miss Bernstein is in the next room. *(To Joe)* Hope that she doesn't take anything else off!
RITA:	Thank you very much.
PADDY:	Don't mention it, madam. *(Leaves with Joe's bag and Rita's coat)*
RITA:	A very polite young man.
JOE:	*(Looking after Paddy)* Young? *(To Rita)* He's just the Group Assistant, I think. Just locks up and brings in the food and helps Miss Bernstein.
RITA:	Oh pity. Are you one of the group?
JOE:	Yes, my name's Joe Fell ... no, ju ... just Joe. There are three other people. They're in there with Miss Bernstein. We're supposed to look around.
RITA:	Not really much to see, is there? Do you like cats?
JOE:	Cats? Well, they're all right. I had one once. It died.
RITA:	Oh poor thing. My husband loved cats. We had twelve of them, you know. We called them after the Twelve Apostles. Judas was our favourite. *(Pause)* I miss him very much.
JOE:	Wh ... what happened to him?
RITA:	He was savaged by dogs.
JOE:	That often happens to cats.
RITA:	No no, Judas is still alive. It was my husband who was savaged by dogs.
JOE:	Oh.
RITA:	Yes, I have a very bad heart condition ever since. Are you a doctor?
JOE:	A doctor? No, not really.
RITA:	Pity. I don't like the idea of being locked up in here without a doctor. I get turns, you know. That's why I always

19

	carry my handbag with me. All my tablets.
JOE:	Ah, I see.
RITA:	I get depressed, you know – since my husband died. I miss him very much. How long is your wife dead?
JOE:	She ... she's not dead.
RITA:	Oh, you're so lucky.
JOE:	No, I ... I mean I'm not married.
RITA:	Ah, pity. We could have shared the emotion of loss. Loss is a terrible thing, you know.
	(Suzy and Roger return)
ROGER:	... do you know that Hegel wrote that this inanimate reaction is still relatively unimportant in terms of personality and conscience ...
SUZY:	Right-on, Roger ... Ah, at last – Rita. It is Rita, isn't it?
RITA:	Yes, are you Miss Bernstein?
SUZY:	Suzy, please. Good to see you. Now can we get going. Oh, this is Roger. Peter and Maureen are looking over the Contemplation Room – right out there – and Joe, I see, you have met. Paddy? Paddy? Paddy!
PADDY:	*(Running in)* Yes, Miss Bernstein?
SUZY:	Everything in order?
PADDY:	Yes, Miss Bernstein.
SUZY:	A quick check of names – Joe, Roger, Rita here; Peter and Maureen outside ... Great, fine. Peter, Maureen! Come in here a moment. *(Peter and Maureen appear)* Okay, now we are all set for our great blast-off into our own world. All set to batten down the hatches, lock up the coop. Paddy is going to seal us all in and he won't appear until 23 hundred hours with our dinner.
RITA:	What time?
SUZY:	Twenty-three hundred hours, Rita.
PETER:	That's nine o'clock, Maureen.
Suzy:	No, eleven, Peter, eleven. Twenty-three hundred. Right?
PETER:	Yes, yes, eleven. Eleven o'clock, Maureen.
RITA:	Eleven o'clock.
SUZY:	Okay. Apart from Paddy's arrival and until he releases us in the morning, we shall live in search – in search of inner knowledge, of ourselves and of others. We have no windows, as you have noticed, the room is soundproof and our only connection with the outside world (in case

	of emergencies) is a telephone which is sealed in that box, right over there.
RITA:	Where?
SUZY:	Right over there, Rita – just for emergencies. *(Laughs)* No phoning loved ones – we will be the whole world.
ROGER:	Ah, the sensory stimulation of incarceration.
RITA:	My husband is dead – he was savaged by dogs.
SUZY:	Fine. So let's take a last look at the outside world, people. In a moment, we will become a family with its own laws, rules and we'll be responsible to no one. It is a great moment, folks, and in Encounter Groups we have a symbolic way of imposing this upon our minds. It is our first group ritual – the long farewell, the beginning of our journey into the unknown chasms of the mind.
ROGER:	Beautiful ... beautiful ...
PADDY:	*(To Joe)* Here it comes now.
SUZY:	So, as a simple symbolism of our being reborn, let's all wave goodbye to Paddy as he returns to his world and we withdraw into our own. It is our rebirth, our appearance from the womb of convention, of discipline, of hypocrisy, of bureaucracy. So wave goodbye to Paddy. This is very symbolic, people. Now goodbye Paddy.
PADDY:	Jaysus!
ROGER:	*Ciao*, Paddy. *Ciao.*
PETER:	Bye-bye, Paddy.
SUZY:	That's it, folks – wave.
MAUREEN:	Goodbye, love.
PADDY:	Good luck, sunshine.
	(Paddy leaves, door is locked. Silence)
PETER:	*(To Maureen)* There was no need for that.
MAUREEN:	For what?
PETER:	For that 'goodbye love'.
MAUREEN:	I was just saying goodbye, for Heaven's sake.
ROGER:	We did this in Oslo, you know.
JOE:	Yeah?
RITA:	Such a nice young man.
SUZY:	*(Springs to life again. Goes to telephone box. Pulls a long string from inside her shirt on which hangs the key to the box)* Okay, fine. Right people, you just relax, relate, communicate while I check the phone here. *(Opens box. Dials number)*

	Four ... Zero ... Zero ... Seven ...
PETER:	*(To Rita)* We didn't really meet – I'm Peter and this is my wife, Maureen.
RITA:	How very nice. Are you a doctor?
SUZY:	Hello Paddy? Paddy? Can you hear me okay?
PETER:	A doctor? No – do I look like a doctor?
MAUREEN:	*(Laughing loudly)* You do, dear – really, you do.
SUZY:	Okay Paddy, you try now. *(Replaces phone)* Phone's okay out, people. Paddy'll ring in now to check.
ROGER:	Excellent organisation. First class.
SUZY:	Thank you Roger.
RITA:	*(To Maureen)* Are *you* a doctor?
MAUREEN:	Oh deary me. *(Laughs)* No, I'm not.
PETER:	Get a grip on yourself, Maureen. *(To Rita)* No, she's not – but you look like a doctor, Rita. Are you? *(Phone rings)*
SUZY:	*(Shouting)* Hello Paddy. Yes fine. You're loud and clear.
RITA:	Oh no, I'm not a doctor – my husband's best friend was a doctor. He was savaged by dogs, you know.
SUZY:	That's fine Paddy ...
PETER:	Dogs? Hey, did you hear that, Roger?
ROGER:	Yes, the phone is working.
PETER:	No, Rita's husband's best friend was savaged by dogs. He was a doctor.
ROGER:	How absolutely dreadful. Did he die?
RITA:	No no, he's still alive – *he* loves dogs. It was my husband who was savaged. He loved cats. I miss him so much.
SUZY:	That's great, Paddy. Okay fine. Bye Paddy.
PETER:	I thought you said it was your husband's best friend ...?
SUZY:	Okay people, now look here. The phone is fine and I'm locking it with this key and I'm keeping the key around my neck like this. *(Puts key back inside her shirt)* So, if I drop dead – ha ha – you'll know where to find it. Okay?
PETER:	*(Quietly to Roger)* I wouldn't mind searching for it ... yabadaba-dooooooo.
RITA:	Yes, I've had a heart condition ever since.
ROGER:	Very understandable Rita – *ce la va sans dire,* as they say.
SUZY:	Fine. Right. Now let's get this show on the road. Everyone sit on the cushions for a moment while I explain a few things.
RITA:	Do I have to sit down?

SUZY: Just for a moment, Rita.

MAUREEN: I'll sit here beside Joe – he looks lonely. Hello Joe.

PETER: Sit here, Maureen – beside me.

MAUREEN: I just thought that Joe ...

PETER: Joe's all right where he is.

MAUREEN: Very well, he just looked lonely, that's all. I'll sit here beside Peter, Joe.

JOE: I ... I don't mind ...

SUZY: Wherever your like, people – just settle down.

RITA: I think I'll sit beside Joe – he likes cats.

ROGER: Ah, relationships building up already, Suzy. I'll stay neutral.

SUZY: Right-on, Roger. Okay, all settle down.

RITA: I have to be careful. It's my heart, you know.

SUZY: Okay, we're all comfortable? Right, now let's be quiet for a moment. Listen to that silence. Close your eyes and listen. Right? Feel that silence spreading over each of us like a heavy mantle, binding us together like a mother's arms, bringing us close like a family. And at the end of this session, we *will* be like a family – a new family. Now, we are children, new to the world, on the first day of our recreation. We are all honesty, we have no masks, no inhibitions, no reason to feel indoctrinated, nothing to conform to – we are free. We are naked, naked to reach out and explore, to ask, to receive, to belong ...

RITA: I like the quiet, Joe – don't you?

SUZY: Just let it linger, folks.

ROGER: Ah yes ... ah yes ...

SUZY: (*Softly*) Anyone want to say anything at this point in time? Express some feeling? Some hope? Anything.

ROGER: I feel ... I wonder ... I want ...

SUZY: Yes, Roger?

ROGER: I wonder if it's better to live alone or to die alone.

SUZY: Fine Roger – that's a good vibration.

RITA: I wonder if my husband hears me.

SUZY: Fine, Rita.

ROGER: Better perhaps to live happily or to die happily.
(*Maureen sniggers*)

SUZY: Maureen? You got a vibration? An impulse?

MAUREEN: No. Nothing.

23

PETER:	Get a grip on yourself, for Heaven's sake.
RITA:	Can ... can he see me ... ?
SUZY:	Fine Rita, we'll probe that.
JOE:	How long is a piece of string ...
	(Maureen laughs)
ROGER:	Is it better to see the world or to live blindly in its image ...
SUZY:	Fine, fine ... anyone else? Anyone? Great, okay. Now, very quietly, let us try our first group exercise. We have been hushed together, tuning our minds – now let us touch. This, people, is a group exercise that accelerates the normal pursuit of discovery. So, let us reach out and touch. Let us try this ...
ROGER:	*(Reaching towards Peter)* Yes yes yes ...
SUZY:	No Roger hold it – not just touching whom we know, but in the darkness of search.
ROGER:	Oh yes, of course – I had forgotten.
SUZY:	*(Rises)* So, easy now, for this initiation I'm going to turn off the light for a moment and we shall stand and move and touch, okay?
RITA:	Do I have to stand up again?
SUZY:	Just to move around quietly. Okay, let's go. Everyone ready? Okay. *(Lights out)* Move around now. Touch.
RITA:	I can't find my handbag ...
SUZY:	Quietly please, silently – okay? Move, touch, move, touch – we are people, right? Crucibles of energy, of hopes, dreams, promises, problems ... reach out ... touch ...
RITA:	Ah, I have it ...
MAUREEN:	*(Giggles)* Is that you, Peter?
PETER:	Oooooops, sorry there ...
RITA:	Where did I leave my tablets ... they don't seem to be ...
SUZY:	Slowly, slowly – concentrate. That's it – reach out, touch ...
MAUREEN:	*(Sudden scream)* Who's that?!
PETER:	Maureen! Are you all right?
MAUREEN	*(Scream and laugh)* Who was that?!
RITA:	Who screamed?
PETER:	Maureen, where are you?
RITA:	Suzy, someone screamed ...
MAUREEN:	Peter, Peter?
	(Lights on. Maureen is beside Peter and Roger. Joe is alone. Rita is searching her handbag)

PETER: What happened, Maureen? What the hell happened?

SUZY: It's okay, folks – all sit down now ...

PETER: Maureen, what happened?

MAUREEN: *(Looking around)* Someone touched ... me. *(Giggles)*

PETER: Where? Who? For God's sake who?

RITA: Ah, I found my tablets – here they are here.

SUZY: It's okay, folks – just an exercise ... settle down now ...

PETER: *(To Roger)* Did you ... did you touch my wife?

ROGER: For heaven's sake, I assure you that I did nothing improper ...

MAUREEN: It's all right Peter – it wasn't anything.

PETER: Then why did you scream? What the hell happened?
            (To Joe) My God, did you ... ?

JOE: What?

SUZY: People, people, people, please. This is supposed to be a
            Touch Therapy ...

ROGER: Yes, of course it is.

PETER: If I find the person who tried to ... to ... to ...

MAUREEN: Come on, Peter, it was nothing. Don't make a scene.

SUZY: Just all sit down, folks. Okay, Roger ... Peter, please ...

RITA: Do I have to sit down again?

PETER: You'd better all be careful ...

SUZY: Fine, Peter, please sit down. Yes, Rita, sit down please for
            the moment.

PETER: You sit down beside me, Maureen.

MAUREEN: *(Annoyed)* I am I am I am I am.

SUZY: Okay now, just a bit of friction there – and that is good.
            That's very good for the session. We need that. Now,
            let's all open up to each other. Let's just talk. Now, who
            wants to start? *(Silence)* Okay, I'm Suzy Bernstein, I come
            from Texaleto in the state of ... eh ... Utah and my greatest
            wish is for the success of this session. I want to admit
            that I'm nervous, anxious for us all. I speak honestly –
            and I want all of you to open up to me and to each other
            ... in such honesty, that, in the end we will all become
            close and intimate and understanding. Now, who'll
            begin?

ROGER: I am Roger ...

SUZY: Fine Roger – you just want to talk to us, right? Okay.

ROGER: I am a name, a body – you see my form, my face, my

25

physique. But I am also an energy, a nebulous undefinable energy. I am me – yet, to me, I am a stranger. I hear echoes – echoes of my own voice repeating back to me everything that I doubt. I see ... I am animal ... I see the fox that waits and watches, I see the horse that stands and prances, I ... I see the elephant that moves in a great, strong sadness ... and I am all of these. I see ...

RITA: Cats?

(Maureen laughs. Peter looks at her)

ROGER: Pardon me?

RITA: Do you see cats?

ROGER: Cats? No, I don't ... I'm trying to say that I relate my search to the animal, to the consciousless beings ... I resent – yet admire – their freedom, their ...

RITA: You must be a vet.

ROGER: A vet? No, I'm an artist, a seeker – a seeker frustrated by the belief that life, however beautiful, is a terminal disease.

RITA: You should be a vet. We used to take our cats to a vet. He loved animals ... and terminal diseases.

ROGER: May I ... may I speak honestly? May I give a here-and-now reaction to the family? We used to do this in Oslo.

SUZY: Sure Roger, just open up. We are all here to listen with great honesty and to help. We are, as you say, your family.

ROGER: Thank you, Suzy. Well, I see a great resentment towards me ...

MAUREEN: Oh no ...

ROGER: Yes I do, Maureen: from Rita with whom I have great difficulty in relating but to whom I want to relate so much, from Joe whom I do not understand because of his silence, from Peter, who I feel, suspects me ...

MAUREEN: Oh no – that's not true ...

PETER: I'll handle this, Maureen I ... I ... eh ... I don't suspect you and ... and I'm sorry if I shouted at you. *(To Suzy)* Is that all right?

SUZY: Great, great, Peter. We had a misunderstanding there and we've conquered it. That's very good for the session.

PETER: To be honest, I know that Maureen is highly-strung and

26

	that, really, is why we're here. Isn't that right Maureen?
MAUREEN:	Yes Peter.
RITA:	I feel that way since my husband died. I take tablets. You should take tablets too, Maureen.
PETER:	No, I decided against that. To be committed to one's work is more important. Isn't that right, Maureen?
MAUREEN:	Yes, Peter.
ROGER:	That's true, Peter – I find consolation in my painting, in the arts, in my exploration of the human body ...
MAUREEN:	Peter builds.
ROGER:	Peter builds?
SUZY:	Who? Peter who?
MAUREEN:	Peter – he builds.
PETER:	I'm a building contractor.
SUZY:	Oh, I get it – you're in real estate.
PETER:	Specialise in select bungalows. Apollo Homes. Exclusive design ...
ROGER:	How artistic. Absolutely beautiful.
PETER:	Thank you. All my bungalows can be built to individual specification – use only quality jig-assembled component parts, all cavity walls; anti-rot, infestation-free timber ... all supplied to individual taste ...
RITA:	Very interesting. Is the market good?
MAUREEN:	He has no trouble selling ...
PETER:	The new wave of buyer in the private sector demands this select, different, individual type and ...
ROGER:	... and you build them. How absolutely magnificent.
MAUREEN:	Peter designed and built our own home ...
ROGER:	A bungalow?
PETER:	Of course – this one is my own, exclusive design. Apollo-plus, I call it.
ROGER:	Ah, Apollo ...
MAUREEN:	You'd love this kitchen, Rita – we had it panelled in pine ...
PETER:	... all natural wood units ...
MAUREEN:	... a copper canopy over the hob unit of the cooker ...
PETER:	Split level cooker, Maureen ...
MAUREEN:	And the wall fabric of the ...
PETER:	The wall fabric of the TV lounge-cum-study was my special choice – hessian. Really hard-wearing yet visually attractive ...

ROGER:	It sounds absolutely magnificent ...
MAUREEN:	Four bedrooms ...
PETER:	Bathroom en suite with the main one, drawing-room lounge with built-in bookshelves and a picture window, dining area off.
MAUREEN:	... television lounge and study ...
PETER:	I said that, Maureen. Ground floor split-level, of course, insulated tiled roofs.
MAUREEN:	... utility room ...
PETER:	... separate WC's, cloakroom.
RITA:	Children's room?
PETER:	A what?
RITA:	A children's room.
PETER:	No, we don't have any children.
RITA:	Ah pity. If my husband and I had children, we would never have had cats. He said that before he was savaged ...
SUZY:	Would you like to have children, Maureen?
MAUREEN:	Well, to be perfectly honest, soon after we married, I ...
PETER:	We decided not to have any children.
SUZY:	Did you really? Don't you like ...?
PETER:	We decided not to have any children.
SUZY:	But you do like children?
PETER:	*(Sternly)* We just decided not to have any.
SUZY:	Oh, I see.
MAUREEN:	Yes, we just decided not to ... have any children. *(Short silence)*
SUZY:	Hey Joe, we haven't heard from you yet.
JOE:	Me?
ROGER:	*(Laughing)* I know he reads cowboy books because he told me that.
RITA:	He isn't a doctor – he told me that.
ROGER:	He's Dr Fell – aren't you Joe?
RITA:	No, he isn't a doctor. He told me so.
MAUREEN:	Can we guess what Joe is ... can we?
PETER:	Well, see what Suzy thinks ...
SUZY:	Why not? That would be a good exercise in speculation – our session must be completely flexible, right? So why not – I'm sure we'll discover how wrong we can be in speculation. Okay by you, Joe?
JOE:	I ... I ... I don't mind.

28

SUZY:	Great. Any guesses?
ROGER:	*(Thoughtfully)* I would say that you have a desk job, Joe. I would speculate that you are an accountant, perhaps, or a ...
PETER:	No no, never. I deal with accountants in my business. No, Joe works with his hands – am I right, Joe?
MAUREEN:	Don't say, Joe, let me guess. You are a carpenter, aren't you?
RITA:	One of my husband's best friends knew a carpenter, but I can't say what he looked like because I never met him.
SUZY:	Well Joe – how are we doing? *(Joe shakes his head)*
ROGER:	Wait – a second guess.
MAUREEN:	No, that's not fair – one guess, Roger.
SUZY:	Shall we let him have a second guess, family?
MAUREEN:	Well, all right ...
SUZY:	Okay with all? Okay, Roger, the family grants you a second guess.
ROGER:	I say that Joe could be a traveller – a salesman ...
PETER:	No, no, never, I know salesmen in my business. Not a salesman, never.
SUZY:	Joe?
JOE:	You're all wr ... wrong.
SUZY:	Did I not say so, people? Now we know how false it is to judge by appearance. So what are you, Joe?
JOE:	*(Stammering badly)* I am a ra ... ra ... radio ann ... ann ... announcer. I re ... re ... read the news on the ra ... radio. *(Silence)*
PETER:	You're joking! *(To Maureen)* He reads the news like that!
RITA:	Really – do you?
MAUREEN:	*(Laughing)* Oh, we're sorry, Joe – but do you honestly? I mean, can you ... well, what I mean is ... is ... I never heard you.
PETER:	Reads the news!
MAUREEN:	I really never heard him.
RITA:	I don't like the news – it's all so depressing and my heart is not strong since my husband was ...
ROGER:	No, this is interesting. I too find it hard to accept, but it *is* possible.
PETER:	Is it?

29

ROGER:	Oh yes, I have known people with a, you know, a speech impediment who can actually speak quite fluently if they are ...
JOE:	*(Shouts)* Well, I don't.
ROGER:	You don't? You mean when you read the news, you don't stammer ...?
JOE:	I don't read the news.
SUZY:	Joe, you said you read the news on the radio.
JOE:	Well, I don't. I can't read the ne ... ne ... news.
PETER:	*(Angry)* Then what are you? This isn't a game. We're all trying to be honest here.
ROGER:	I said what I was – I was being quite honest.
RITA:	So was I.
PETER:	Well, what are you?
MAUREEN:	Perhaps Joe would prefer not to tell us.
PETER:	Not tell us? The what's he going to do? Just sit there and listen? Of course he'll have to tell us.
ROGER:	Yes Joe, of course you must open up and ...
PETER:	Come on, tell us.
ROGER:	We are your family, remember.
JOE:	*(Quietly)* I'm a trans-Atlantic pilot.
RITA:	A what? What did he say?
PETER:	He said he was a pilot.
JOE:	*(Louder)* And I'm a rat-catcher.
PETER:	A what? – you're a what?
JOE:	And I'm a doctor and I'm a thinker ...
PETER:	Wait a minute!
JOE:	*(Louder)* and I'm a cat-lover and a builder of exclusive bungalows *(Shouts louder)* and I ... I'm the man who puts the cracks into cream crackers and the ... the ...
SUZY:	Hold it, Joe ...
JOE:	... and I'm the promised Messiah, I'm the riddle of the Sphinx, I ... I'm the Salt of the Earth, I ... I'm Rocky Marciano ... I'm ... I'm everything that crawls, flies, walks, shuffles, staggers, ... I'm ... I'm ... I'm ... *(Silence)*
PETER:	Oh my God. *(Maureen laughs)* Shut up, Maureen – get a grip on yourself.
SUZY:	*(Controlled)* Joe, do you want to tell us? *(Silence)* Would you like to tell me? Or anyone? *(Silence)* What would

	you like to do?
JOE:	I'd like to go the jacks.
SUZY:	The what, Joe?
ROGER:	He means the loo.
Suzy:	Oh sure, sure. You know where it is. You don't have to ask. It's okay, Joe – go ahead. It's okay.
	(Joe leaves)
PETER:	My God, are we safe in here with him? Are you all right Maureen?
MAUREEN:	Yes, of course I am.
PETER:	And you wanted to sit beside him. My God!
MAUREEN:	I just said that to be sociable.
PETER:	Sociable? With him? Well, you just sit there now.
MAUREEN:	I *am* sitting here.
RITA:	He was shouting – I don't like shouting. My husband would never shout.
SUZY:	Okay, okay – now how do we react? That's the point now, people. This is great for the session. How can we help – what does the family see?
ROGER:	I see a great confusion – a mixture of blues and yellows, jagged lines. I see great layers emerging. Dostoievski says – 'He who has a predilection for abstract deduction is ready to distort the truth for his own advantage'. I am warned by this and I try to see ...
PETER:	I see a nut case! We're not safe locked in here with him!
RITA:	He said he wasn't a doctor and then he said he was ...
ROGER:	A real Dr Fell perhaps – 'I do not like thee Dr Fell, and why it is I cannot tell ...'
PETER:	I can tell why I don't like him – he's nuts!
SUZY:	Look people, we can help – we must remember that. For the sake of the session, we must try to understand, to console, to relate, to ... *(Joe enters)* ... Oh Joe, come in. You okay?
JOE:	*(Sits beside Rita)* Yes, I'm grand. I want to apologise.
SUZY:	That's okay, Joe. Is it okay, people?
ROGER:	Indeed it is.
JOE:	I'm very sorry.
SUZY:	Don't worry, Joe – we can sort everything out. We all make mistakes, but with honesty and openness, the session solves everything. So don't worry about it.

PETER:	*(To Maureen)* It's all right now – don't worry.
JOE:	I'm an electrician.
RITA:	Ah, that's nice.
PETER:	It's your current occupation! Get it? Current occupation – electrician.
SUZY:	Good joke, Peter.
JOE:	*(Smiling, relaxed)* Yes, that's good.
ROGER:	Joe, would you like to tell us exactly what you do – or would you prefer ... ?
JOE:	No no – I sit in a little office, at a brown desk and wait for the phone to ring for people to tell me that their per ... percolator won't work or their toaster is broken and they can't have their breakfast ...
ROGER:	Yes, I understand ...
JOE:	... or that their electric blanket won't get warm and that they can't sleep or that their shaver or their hairdryer won't work and they can't go out – and then I get into my little red van, drive over to them and fix whatever is wrong. That's all.
SUZY:	That's great, Joe. Fine.
ROGER:	Ah, you work at night, then?
JOE:	Week on, week off – yes.
MAUREEN:	And you like your work?
JOE:	It's interesting, sometimes.
PETER:	Especially when you've got to fix an electric blanket, eh? Chance of a bit of yabadaba-dooooo.
MAUREEN:	Peter! Don't be rude!
PETER:	I'm not rude – it's a joke.
JOE:	No, nothing like that.
MAUREEN:	Of course not. Joe's not like that.
ROGER:	So there we are. *Quod erat demonstrandum.*
SUZY:	Do you want to say something to Joe, Rita?
RITA:	Yes – you're not a doctor then, are you?
JOE:	No, I told you – I'm a pilot.
PETER:	Holy Christ!
	(Silence)
SUZY:	*(Controlled)* A pilot, Joe? I thought you said that you were an electrician?
JOE:	Oh yes, I'm sorry – I'm an electrician. Not a pilot. Or a doctor.

SUZY:	Okay, people – great. We've broken the ice, right? We all know each other a little better now, right? We've had a sudden sharing in a here-and-now situation, we've got some great reaction, we've sorted it out and that has brought us closer. Yet, we still wear masks, don't we? Some of us, I feel, are still showing a face to the world. So why don't we try our second Therapy exercise – and just regard each other for a moment ...
ROGER:	Ah yes, we did this in Oslo. This is good.
RITA:	Do I have to stand up again?
SUZY:	Just for a moment, Rita – then we'll break for private communication. So will we try it? Just stand up, don't say a word, don't touch – just stare each other in the face. Get it? We call it eyeballing in the States.
	(Suzy stands up)
PETER:	Are you going to turn off the light again?
SUZY:	No Peter, we'll leave the light on for this. Let's try it, slowly.
	(All stand)
ROGER:	Super. Hello Peter.
SUZY:	Silently, please. Don't touch – just look.
ROGER:	Oh yes, of course.
	(All move around – staring each other)
SUZY:	Let that look linger, folks. Move around, Peter – that's it. Gaze down into the soul. Don't hide anything. Just relax and let your eyes communicate. *(Pause)* Quietly now. Great. Feel that silent discovery ...
	(As they finish, Joe and Maureen stand gazing at each other)
PETER:	Eh, Maureen ...?
SUZY:	It's okay, Peter.
	(All watch in silence)
PETER:	Maureen ...?
ROGER:	Shhhhhhhhhh ...
RITA:	They look nice, don't they?
ROGER:	They're searching the hidden chasms of the mind ...
SUZY:	Quiet please – let them discover ...
PETER:	Maureen ...?
SUZY:	Easy Peter – let them be ...
PETER:	*(Shouts)* Maureen, for God's sake. *(Disengages them)* *(To Joe)* What the hell are you at? This is my wife, you

33

	know.
SUZY:	Hey Peter, easy – this is an exercise in discovery.
PETER:	Well, I tell you what I discovered – he can't be trusted. Not with the truth and not with my wife. My God, Maureen!
MAUREEN:	I'm sorry, Peter – but I didn't hear you.
PETER:	How bloody convenient – as usual.
MAUREEN:	Now Peter, don't start that.
PETER:	I didn't start it – you started it.
ROGER:	It's just an exercise, Peter – a discovery.
PETER:	Well, ask him what *he* discovered.
SUZY:	Joe?
JOE:	What?
SUZY:	Peter asks what you discovered.
JOE:	*(Pause)* That I can't be trusted ... at all.
MAUREEN:	*(Laughs)* O deary me ...
PETER:	Get a grip on yourself, for God's sake.
ROGER:	Well, I discovered in Rita a great sadness. A blue – yes, a blue. It helps me to relate to her now. I see a great loss and I feel a need to reach out to her ...
RITA:	Do you really? I've had this great sadness since ...
JOE:	... he was savaged by dogs.
RITA:	Yes, that's right, Joe.
SUZY:	See? The layers are being stripped away, people. We've had our first general symposium – now it's time for private communication. We are now free to do as we please. We can sit here and develop our relationships or we can retire to the Contemplation Room. We are free for a while – get it?
JOE:	What time is it?
SUZY:	Time doesn't count here, Joe. Why do you ask?
JOE:	No ... No reason.
SUZY:	Fine. We'll all reassemble before dinner okay?
ROGER:	Would you like to sit here with me, Rita?
RITA:	Oh yes – did I tell you about my husband?
PETER:	I want to talk to you, Maureen – privately.
MAUREEN:	For Heaven's sake, Peter!
PETER:	Yes, for Heaven's sake!
SUZY:	Joe, are you going to join us?
JOE:	*(Stands up)* Eh ... no.
PETER:	What are you going to do now?

34

JOE: *(Moves towards Contemplation Room)* I think I'll just con-
template ...
PETER: My God ... !

LIGHTS OUT.
END OF SCENE ONE, ACT ONE.

Act One

Scene Two

When lights come up, Roger, Maureen, Suzy and Rita are talking. Peter is examining the walls. Joe is still in the Contemplation Room.

ROGER: Ah, but the wish to be one's self does not occur – for only self known is empty and must be filled from the outside.

MAUREEN: Oh Roger, a bit slower, please. You say that we prefer to be someone other than ourselves?

SUZY: To be a pseudonym, you mean.

ROGER: Yes, that too – Van Den Haag says that we long to impersonate, to get a name – better to be a pseudonym than to remain nameless; better a borrowed character than none; better to regard ourselves ...

PETER: That's a load of rubbish.

SUZY: Sorry Peter – what was that?

PETER: *(Tapping the wall)* That plaster coat – covers a lot of sloppy work ...

SUZY: Really?

PETER: No buyer would touch that nowadays – all very fine as a hotch-potch job, but to the select buyer – no.

MAUREEN: Yes, that's true, Peter.

ROGER: As I was saying, de-individualisation should not be viewed as a grim, deliberate or coercive process – it is always, as in all ...

PETER: And whoever bricked up that window should be shot.

RITA: Shot?

SUZY: Okay folks, we can leave it there for a moment – time for our next session before dinner.

ROGER: *(To Maureen)* It's simply a conclusion that, of real identity, we have no measure ...

PETER: If I put up a wall like that, I wouldn't sell ...

SUZY: Okay fine – that's it for the present. Joe? Joe? *(Silence)* Would you come out now, Joe – we're having a general session. Joe?

PETER: What the hell is he doing in there, anyway?

RITA: I'd forgotten about Joe.

ROGER: He's probably contemplating ...

PETER: Contemplating what?

JOE: *(Appears)* Sor ... sorry. I don't have my toothbrush.

ROGER: Your toothbrush?

JOE: I'll have to get it out of my bag when Pa ... Paddy opens the door.

SUZY: I thought you had one, Joe.

ROGER: Yes, you did have one – I saw it.

RITA: Yes, I saw it too. It was green.

PETER: No, that was mine. Mine is green. Maureen's is orange.

RITA: *(To Roger)* Oranges are good for you – they contain calcium.

SUZY: Have you mislaid it, Joe?

JOE: No.

ROGER: Then where is it?

JOE: It's in my bag. I'll have to get it when Pa ... Paddy opens the door.
(Silence)

SUZY: Look Joe, we can sort this out – we've been sorting lots of things out while you've been in there – haven't we, family? *(General agreement)* Now, what colour was it?

JOE: Black.

PETER: Black? A black toothbrush? I never saw anyone with a black toothbrush.

ROGER: It was a primary colour, I think – I think I remember a yellow one.

MAUREEN: Yes yes – it was yellow. I remember because yellow is so near to orange and mine is orange and Peter's is pink.

PETER: No, mine is green.

MAUREEN: No, pink – yours is pink.

PETER: It's green, Maureen – I know the colour of my own bloody toothbrush.

RITA: Mine is blue. I like blue – it's restful.

ROGER: Depends on the shade, Rita. A sky blue is rather pleasant.

RITA: That's what mine is – sky blue. It's very pleasant.

MAUREEN: Shall we all look for Joe's toothbrush then?

PETER: Look for it? Why?

MAUREEN: For fun – what else?

SUZY: Good idea – that's co-operation within the family. Come on, Peter.

PETER: This is stupid – bloody stupid – looking for his ... his toothbrush.
            (All stand)

ROGER: What colour are we looking for?

MAUREEN: Ah, that's the game. I say yellow, Joe says black, Rita says green.

PETER: Mine is green.

SUZY: Okay then, we'll give it two minutes of hard searching, people. Hard searching. *(All begin to search)* Our whole session is a search, right?

ROGER: *(From Contemplation Room)* Nothing in the bathroom – no blacks at all ...

RITA: *(Lifting cushions)* I wish I could search more – I have to be careful, you know.

ROGER: Just try a little – leave no stone unturned ...

MAUREEN: ... And no turn unstoned ...

SUZY: *(Laughing)* Come on, all try harder ...

MAUREEN: *(Sings)* Come out little toothbrush, show your colour, Come out little toothbrush ...
            (Unnoticed, Joe takes a white toothbrush from his pocket and holds it aloft)

SUZY: Come on, Peter – search ...

RITA: I thought I saw it ... no, it was nothing ...

SUZY: One minute to go, folks and then we quit ...

MAUREEN: No no, we'll find it ...

PETER: *(Seeing Joe)* Hey, what's that?

JOE: A toothbrush.

RITA: It's white.

ROGER: Is it yours Joe?

JOE: Yes.

PETER: How many have you got?

SUZY: Joe, I thought you said a black toothbrush – that's white.

JOE: I do have a black one – it's in my bag outside. I'll have to get it when Pa ... Paddy opens the door.
            (Silence)

PETER: Then what are we all looking for?

JOE: I don't know.

MAUREEN: *(Laughs)* Well, it was fun anyway.

38

PETER: Holy Christ!

SUZY: Well okay, folks – that was an interesting, immediate exercise. Now let's just sit and talk before dinner.

ROGER: Excellent idea.
           (All sit)

SUZY: So who wants to begin. Who wants to give a reaction to our new relationships ...

PETER: I'd like to know why he goes on like that. Hiding ... not talking..

SUZY: Right. Do you feel that a barrier has been created?

PETER: I certainly do.

SUZY: Well, I'm sure Joe had his reasons for wanting to be alone, to be at peace with his thoughts. Right, Joe?

JOE: I didn't want to upset anyone anymore.

ROGER: Oh, that's all in the past, Joe. We're all friends now. Rita and I have been very close – and Peter and Maureen too, of course ...

SUZY: Right-on, Roger. So, just sit here with us Joe and talk. Open up. *(Silence)* Roger, you were telling me about your friend, remember? A lovely story – I'm sure that Joe, and the others, would like to share it.

RITA: I love stories – is it a nice story?

ROGER: It's a sad, blue, soft story. It affected me deeply but I learned from it.

SUZY: We're all learning tonight – right, Maureen, Peter?

PETER: We are all right!

MAUREEN: Of course we are.

SUZY: Right, okay Roger – just as you told me.

ROGER: Well, I was young, at boarding school and Tom was my chum, my best friend.

RITA: That's nice. Tom – that's a nice name.

ROGER: We shared everything. We sat together in class, we went for long walks in the afternoon, we roomed together ... we ... were close. It's hard to explain: you would have to have seen us together, to hear our laughter, to feel our silences, to know how much we depended upon each other, to really understand. I ... I never thought that we could be anything but friends – until that summer when we parted for holidays. Tom was getting the train and I walked with him to the station and we said goodbye. I stood on the platform and he leaned from the carriage window and we stood there talking little things, farewell things ...

MAUREEN: I know. *(To Peter)* When you went to Kerry to inspect the housing site – like that. Do you remember I went to the station? Do you remember ...?

PETER: *(Stiffly)* Of course I do.

RITA: My husband used to be like that too.

ROGER: Well, something happened to the train that day – it was broken or the signals went wrong – anyway it didn't move. It just stayed there in the station and I stood on the platform and Tom was leaning out towards me and ... then we were saying nothing. We didn't even look at each other, after a while. I was embarrassed – no, annoyed – at our silence, at our uncomfortable silence and I knew that he, like me, was just praying that the damn train would move. But it didn't. It just stayed there. It just stayed ...

SUZY: You had said everything, right?

ROGER: Yes, yes – but it was more than that. We both felt it. It wasn't that we had just said our goodbyes, it was as if ... as if we had said everything ... for ever. We were sudden strangers – and I could not even remember what had ever brought us close. I couldn't remember a single thing that we had in common. I couldn't even remember what we had lost.

RITA: My husband had a friend who was a doctor and *he* had a friend like that. But they had a lot in common ... they were never strangers ...

ROGER: Well, Tom and I *were* strangers – from that moment. And when the train eventually moved, he just nodded and I turned away and ran down that platform. I didn't even wait to see if he waved – I'm sure he didn't – I'm sure he hated me in that instant.

RITA: I'm sure he didn't ...

ROGER: He never wrote – all through that summer, he never wrote and ... and I knew that I would never see him again. I knew – and I knew why.

MAUREEN: I think you should have written, Roger.

ROGER: No no, it would have been no good.

40

MAUREEN: A new relationship could have developed *(To Peter)* like
when you were in Kerry and I wrote to you every day.
Do you remember?

PETER: That was different, Maureen.

MAUREEN: Was it?

PETER: *(Softly)* We were married, for God's sake.

ROGER: Nothing would ever have been the same again ... People
are like that – well, I believed for many years that they
were and, in that time, I learned that only the animal –
without deep feelings – can escape this. I believed that,
for a long time.
(Silence)

SUZY: So what did you do, Roger?

ROGER: Well, I have tried ... I have really tried to re-discover people ... and myself. I have succeeded and I have failed.
But *sic itur ad astra* – such is the way of the stars. My fail-
ure has been shown in my complete impersonal dedica-
tion to the arts: I am narcissian, you know – I am, I know
I am. My success began when I started Group Therapy.
And I have found that I'm not alone – that there were
others ...

RITA: I am miserable too.

ROGER: Yes, and I'd like to relate to you, Rita ...

RITA: Would you?

ROGER: I really would. I really would.

SUZY: You see, we all seek happiness and understanding
through communications and it is there for those who
just open out, honestly. I'm sure you see that in this session, Roger.

MAUREEN: I think that Joe is very lonesome. Are you Joe?

JOE: Me? No.

MAUREEN: I feel that you are.

PETER: If he says he's not, he's not. Get a grip on yourself.

ROGER: I wonder, Peter. Did you ever lose, Joe? I mean, lose as I
lost Tom. Did that ever happen to you?

JOE: *(Quietly)* I don't want to upset anyone anymore.

SUZY: Oh, you won't – we are all your family and we want to
hear of your hopes, your plans, your dreams.

JOE: My dreams ...?

ROGER: Just tell us, Joe. We can help.

41

JOE: I had a cat once ... when I was young.

SUZY: Good Joe, tell us about it.

ROGER: *(To Rita)* You'll be interested in this, Rita – you like cats.

RITA: Was it a black cat, Joe – Judas was black, you know.

JOE: It was blue. I gave it milk every day and it was big and fat with thick glossy fur and black eyes and in the evening I would sit at the fire and it would cuddle at my feet and purr and stretch on its back and I would run my hand over its belly and ...

RITA: Joe? It couldn't have been a blue cat. There are no blue cats.

JOE: No, it was black – like my toothbrush. I remember.

PETER: Christ!

RITA: *(To Roger)* Like Judas, Judas was black with thick fur ...

MAUREEN: What was your cat's name, Joe?

JOE: It was ... it was Maureen. I called him Maureen. I loved her very much.

MAUREEN: *(Laughs)* Oh deary me.

PETER: Wait a minute. Why did you have to call her Maureen?

ROGER: No Peter, this could explain a lot. This is interesting.

PETER: What's interesting?

ROGER: This is. This could be an association of names. I had that once with a ... with a person I knew. Names haunt like smells, like music – they all become associations.

SUZY: Do you still have your cat, Joe?

JOE: No. *(Pause)* No, when I was fifteen, I took her out, I carried her under my coat, along the road, up the hill to the railway bridge. I kept saying to her 'I love you, Maureen; I love you, Maureen; I love you Maureen ...'

PETER: Get on with your story, for God's sake – what happened?

JOE: Nothing happened.

ROGER: You brought her home again?

RITA: We used to do that with our twelve cats – our apostles – take them out for a walk. Only we used to go in our car. My husband used to drive. He was a wonderful driver.

SUZY: Did you bring her home again Joe?
(Silence)

JOE: I climbed the wall beside the bridge and carried her down the embankment to the railway line to wait for the train. We sat in the grass waiting for the train. She was purring, I was sleepy *(Pause)* and after the train passed, I carried her home again.

ROGER: Why did you do that, Joe?

JOE: Because I loved her.

PETER: Loved her? She must have been terrified by the train, for God's sake.

RITA: Our cats were never terrified in the car..

SUZY: Did you often do that Joe?

JOE: No, just once.

ROGER: Ah, I see ...

JOE: I buried her in the garden beside the wall.

MAUREEN: Alive? You buried her alive?

PETER: Oh suffering Christ!

JOE: No no – she was dead.

MAUREEN: Ah, she died?

RITA: Did she die?

JOE: Yes, she died when I threw her under the train ...

MAUREEN: You threw her under the ... ?

JOE: I just held her out as the train approached, let her see it, and she kicked and struggled and screamed ...

RITA: *(Holding her chest)* Roger, I don't like this ...

ROGER: Quite. I really think we should ...

JOE: ... and as the noise came nearer, I could see the driver's face, looking at me, and I just held her out ...

PETER: For Christ sake!

JOE: ... and tossed her under the wheels ...

RITA: No no – stop it ... I don't want to hear ...

MAUREEN: Joe, I don't really believe that you really ...

JOE: ... and Maureen screamed – just once – a long scream above the rattle of the wheels.

PETER: Shut up, shut up you mad bastard. *(Rises)*

SUZY: *(Rises)* Okay, okay that's enough. Settle down.

RITA: My heart! *(Searches her bag)* I don't feel well ... my pills, my pills ...

ROGER: Are you all right? I'll get some water. *(Dashes to Contemplation Room)*

JOE: ... and there was blood all along the line ...

PETER: For Christ's sake – shut up!

JOE: ... and the grass was speckled with blood ...

43

SUZY: Enough! That's enough ... that's enough!
JOE: *(Shouts)* And then I woke up!
           (Silence. Roger dashes in with a glass of water)
MAUREEN: You woke? It was all a dream? A nightmare?
RITA: A dream?
ROGER: A dream? What was all a dream?
PETER: He says it was all a bloody dream, the whole thing.
RITA: A dream. It was a dream, wasn't it, Joe?
           (Silence)
ROGER: The water, Rita.
RITA: No, I'm all right now. It was a dream.
SUZY: Joe, was that a dream?
JOE: Yes. When I woke, I was sitting on the embankment and
           a sparrow was singing and it was quiet and peaceful and
           I was looking up along the line and the sun was shining
           on the rails and this little ladybird jumped onto the back
           of my hand and I watched it and it was so peaceful ...
           and warm ...
RITA: And ... where was ... where was Maureen?
PETER: Maureen my arse!
MAUREEN: Peter, listen.
SUZY: Where was your cat, Joe?
JOE: With me. Purring. Years later she died – savaged by dogs
           – and I buried her in the garden.
PETER: For the love of God, do you know what you're talking
           about ...
JOE: A dream. I'm sorry *(Stammer returns)* I ... I'm sorry about
           your heart, Rita ... I'm so ... sorry if I upset you Maureen
           ... I'm sorry if you're ann ... annoyed, Roger ... Peter, I'm
           sorry ...
RITA: It was a horrible story, Joe.
ROGER: It most certainly was.
JOE: You asked me ... you all asked me. You asked me for my
           dreams.
SUZY: No those kind ... okay, okay, settle down, folks.
ROGER: Well, I must say that I found it very upsetting. However,
           we are a family – as Suzy says – and we shall try to help
           you, Joe.
JOE: Yes. I'm so sorry.
SUZY: That's okay, now, Joe.

JOE: It was a dream – but it was true – a true dream.

ROGER: You should have said it was a dream – even if it *was* true.

JOE: It *was* true – as true as ... as ... as ... As true as I'm an electrician.

PETER: But *are* you a bloody electrician?

SUZY: Now Peter, he said he was ...

PETER: He said a lot of things. *(To Joe)* What's the speed of light?

JOE: The what?

PETER: Speed! The speed of light! What is it? If you are an electrician you'll know that.

SUZY: Now Peter, hold it – we don't go checking out everyone. We rely on honesty.

MAUREEN: Yes, that's fair, Peter.

PETER: Fair? For Christ's sake, Maureen!

JOE: 186,000 miles per second.

SUZY: There. Is that right, Peter?

PETER: I suppose so.

JOE: And the voltage multiplied by the amperage gives watts.

MAUREEN: *(Laughing)* What's watts?

SUZY: Yeah, what what. Okay great – we're all together again. The session is going just great.

RITA: Was your cat really savaged by dogs?

JOE: Yes, she was.

RITA: That's terrible. Just like my husband. Do you take tablets?

JOE: Tablets?

RITA: For your nerves.

MAUREEN: I'm sure he doesn't.

JOE: I don't.

RITA: You should, really.

PETER: Bloody cyanide tablets!

MAUREEN: Peter!

(Key is turned in door. Paddy enters with a tray)

SUZY: *(Springs to life)* Ah food! Hi Paddy. Okay people time-out now for eats. Let's just relax, relate, communicate as we eat. We've passed the first session – we've learned a lot and we're still learning from each other. The therapy is really going great ... really great ...

PADDY: Will I put it inside?

SUZY: Yeah right, Paddy. Into the Contemplation Room.

PADDY: Very well, Miss. *(Paddy smiles at Joe as he goes)*

JOE: *(To all)* I'm really sorry.

ROGER: It's perfectly all right now, Joe. I'm starving.

SUZY: Sure, sure Joe – come on, folks. Ah, you can get your black toothbrush now, Joe if you wish ...

PETER: *(To Maureen)* Come on, come on.

MAUREEN: *(Laughing)* I'm coming, I'm coming, I am coming!

SUZY: Paddy? Paddy? Paddy! *(Paddy runs out)* Paddy, Joe wants his bag for a moment, okay?

Paddy: Oh right Miss – this way sunshine.
           (As everyone leaves, Joe waits for Paddy to get the bag. Looks around the room. Goes to phone box)

PADDY: *(With Joe's bag)* Here you are sunshine – leaving already?

JOE: No, just get ... get ... getting a toothbrush.

PADDY: Thought you got that earlier.

JOE: *(Searching bag)* No, I forgot it.

PADDY: Fair enough – you work away there while I get the other trays. How's it going anyway – did Victoria get them off her yet? *(Carries tray through)*

JOE: *(Searching)* No, nothing li ... like that.

PADDY: Glad to hear it – that'd put you off women for life.
           (Passing by) Find that toothbrush?

JOE: Yes, I got it. It was at the bottom. Will I leave the bag outside?

PADDY: *(With another tray)* Oh right. Just put it in the closet outside.
           (Joe leaves with bag)

ROGER: *(From room)* Who will say grace?

MAUREEN: *(From room)* I will – 'grace' – there, I've said it.
           (General laughter)

JOE: *(Returning – meets Paddy from room)* I put it in the closet.

PADDY: Right sunshine – hey tell us, was I right about them?

JOE: Well, they're not very hon ... honest. We just had a se .. session in which we were all supposed to ...

PADDY: Don't tell me sunshine – I've had enough troubles. Went home to find one of the chiselers fell off the shed. The whole side of his arm scraped. Lucky it wasn't broke. And the bleedin' telly is on the blink – and the wife's got one of her headaches. Jaysus, I'm telling you, if this goes

46

	on, I'll be in here myself next week.
JOE:	Ah, you wouldn't fi ... fi ... fit in here.
PADDY:	Jas, I don't know.
JOE:	Did you find out about Texaleto?
PADDY:	About what ...? ah, Texale ...? ... No, you didn't tell me ...
JOE:	Doesn't matter. When are you coming back?
PADDY:	Back? Oh back at 7.00 am sharp to turn youse all loose, God help us. Better get going now *(Shouts)* I'm off now, Miss Bernstein.
SUZY:	*(From room)* Okay Paddy, see you at 700 hours. Thanks a million. Come on, Joe – the food's getting cold.
PADDY:	Not a bleedin' wave this time. All right, sunshine – see you in the morning.
JOE:	Yes, goodbye Paddy. *(Waves to Paddy)*
	(Paddy leaves. Door is locked. Joe waits. Goes to telephone box again)
SUZY:	*(From room)* Joe! Joe are you coming? We're eating here like bears. *(Laughter)*
MAUREEN:	*(From room)* Come on, Joe – I've kept a doughnut for you. *(More laughter)*
JOE:	All right, I'm coming ...
	(Joe quickly reaches out, holds the phone flex and pulls it from the wall. Conceals the loose part in the socket. Glances around the room)
SUZY:	Joe! Joe, what's keeping you?
JOE:	I'm coming. *(Goes to room)* Here I am. *(Closes door)*

END OF ACT ONE
CURTAIN

Act Two

Scene One

Suzy, Roger, Rita and Maureen are sitting, talking. Peter and Joe are off-stage in the Contemplation Room.

MAUREEN: *(Laughing)* Come on, Rita – you're not trying.

RITA: I am I am – I can *see* my twelve little pussy-cats – it's putting names on them that is difficult. Now – Peter, Andrew, James, John, Philip ... Bartholomew ... oh, dear ... Philip ... Bartholomew ... Bartholomew ...

ROGER: Ah Rita, you have forgotten. Yet, *et spes non fracta* ...

RITA: No no – I haven't forgotten – I'm just trying to picture them: I see Bartholomew now, a big lad Bartholomew, proud – now, who's that behind you, Bartholomew? Ah, Thomas. How could I forget little Thomas.

MAUREEN: That's eight. Come on – four to go.

RITA: Four to go. Thomas ... Thomas ...

ROGER: You said him, Rita.

RITA: Yes, I know. John, Philip, Bartholomew, Thomas ... Matthew?

SUZY: Matthew. Right. Three more.

PETER: *(Shouts from room)* Well, what the hell's that got to do with you?

RITA: Bartholomew, Thomas, Matthew ...

MAUREEN: *(Looking towards the room)* Peter?

RITA: No, I said Peter.

MAUREEN: Peter is something the matter? Joe?

SUZY: It's okay, Maureen – they're just sorting something out, I guess. Let them be.

MAUREEN: They've been in there for ages.

ROGER: It's good to see Joe opening-up. He was very quiet at the start.

SUZY: Joe is an introvert – needs a lot of sympathy.

PETER: *(From room)* I said No – that's final No!

RITA: Thomas ... and Matthew ...

ROGER: Pity we're missing it, really – I'd honestly like to know

48

RITA:	what's so important in there.
RITA:	It's James.
MAUREEN:	Who is James?
RITA:	He's the striped one.
MAUREEN:	Oh, the cats.
PETER:	*(Shouts)* Rubbish! Absolute rubbish!
RITA:	... and Thaddeus ... James, Thaddeus ...
PETER:	*(Shouts)* No, we won't ask her – we bloody well won't.
SUZY:	Hi, you two – is that a private exchange or will you come out and let the family join in?
MAUREEN:	I'm going to see. *(Runs to Contemplation Room)*
RITA:	How many is that, Roger?
ROGER:	Oh, I don't know, Rita ... I'm sorry, I haven't been counting. Suzy, how many was that?
SUZY:	Was it eleven?
ROGER:	Yes, that's right. Eleven. One to go.
RITA:	One to go. Let me see now. My husband, you know, could name them like a song. Where is pussy number twelve? Simon! Simon, you bad cat – hiding from my memory.
ROGER:	Bravo Rita – that's the famous twelve.
MAUREEN:	*(From room)* Tell me, Peter, tell me ...
PETER:	No, no, no, it is nothing. This ... this ... mad bastard ... sorry love ... come on, we're going out ... *(Maureen appears)*
MAUREEN:	*(Looking back)* I'd like to know what he said.
PETER:	*(Appearing)* It was nothing ... a load of shhh ... load of rubbish.
ROGER:	Hello there.
SUZY:	Hi people, can the family help?
ROGER:	We sit in the hope of being asked.
PETER:	*(Sitting)* It's private.
ROGER:	It shouldn't be. Not to the family – not within the circle.
PETER:	Well it bloody-well is.
MAUREEN:	Peter! Don't talk like that, please.
PETER:	I bloody well will talk like that.
RITA:	Judas!
PETER:	What the hell do you mean by that?
RITA:	Judas – he's another. I forgot Judas.
SUZY:	Rita has been naming her twelve cats for us.

49

PETER: Oh, for Christ's sake – not again.

MAUREEN: Peter! What has annoyed you so much?

PETER: It's not me – it's that fool out there with his lies and ... his games and ... his bloody insinuations.

ROGER: Tell us. Peter – we can help, we really can. Our arms are open, our minds are awakened, we sit in hope to hear you *verbatim et litteratim* ...

PETER: Will you cut that out – that fancy, educated talk. He's no right to say ... what he said.

MAUREEN: What did he say?

PETER: Never mind!

SUZY: *(Controlled)* Peter, when we're strung-up, up-tight, we cannot communicate and our problems just grow and grow out of all proportion. So, unless you really feel that we shouldn't know, why not just unwind and tell us your problem.

PETER: It's not my problem – it's his. *(Indicates room)*

JOE: *(Appearing)* Hello family.

ROGER: Ah, welcome Joe.

PETER: Don't sit near me – I'm warning you.

MAUREEN: Peter!

PETER: And don't sit near her. *(Indicates Maureen)*

MAUREEN: Oh, for Heaven's sake.

PETER: Yes, for Heaven's sake.

SUZY: Sit here, Joe – beside Rita. Okay Rita?

RITA: That's thirteen apostles – thirteen cats, Judas makes thirteen. Did I count them properly, Roger? Oh sorry, Suzy – what did you say?

SUZY: Joe is going to sit here beside you – that okay?

RITA: Oh yes, do sit here, Joe. Can you name the twelve apostles?

JOE: Yes.

RITA: Can you really?

JOE: *(Quietly)* Yes. Peter, Andrew, James, John, Philip, Bartholomew, Thomas, James and Thaddeus, Matthew, Simon and Judas.

SUZY: That is fantastic, Joe.

ROGER: Yes indeed – *mirabile, mirabile*. Congratulations.

JOE: Thanks *(Pause)* And there's no record of any of them having any children.

PETER: *(Jumping up)* Christ! I'll kill you if you don't shut your ...

MAUREEN: Peter, sit down. He didn't say anything.

PETER: I know what he's saying – and I'm not going to sit here and listen ...

SUZY: Easy now, easy. Don't get up-tight. Keep it cool. Now what's the problem? *(Peter sits)* Come on.

PETER: Change the subject.

SUZY: Joe, what's this all about? Tell the family. What did you say?

JOE: Me? I just said that they had no children.

PETER: Leave it at that now – everyone knows we have no children. We decided not to ...

JOE: I said the apostles had no children – not you.
              (Silence)

MAUREEN: Was that it, Peter? Was it? About us having no children?

PETER: Part of it ...

SUZY: Ah Peter, that's fine. Take it easy. We know all about that – we've had that. That's okay.

PETER: You know too much – all of you. And it's all his bloody fault ...

JOE: Me?

ROGER: Look, Peter, you're hyper-sensitive about this – and I can understand. It's very common – people become hyper-sensitive about things that other people don't even notice.

SUZY: That is so true, you know.

ROGER: I had a friend – a charming person – who had a mole on his ... her leg and, do you know, she never went out swimming. She would never take off her clothes in public – never! He thought that nobody ever saw anything *except* the mole – but nobody ever noticed her damn mole. *(Pause)* Look, talking of children, Rita had none – but she's not sensitive about it. Are you Rita?

RITA: I had twelve – but I've counted thirteen now.

PETER: Holy Christ!

ROGER: No – children, Rita, not cats.

RITA: Oh no, we didn't have any children ... I would have liked a daughter like Suzy or Maureen ... or a son like you, Roger ... or Peter ...

JOE: Or me?

51

RITA:	Of course, Joe – or you.
PETER:	A fine son he'd make!
RITA:	Yes, a fine son ... or Roger or a daughter like Maureen or Suzy or ...
MAUREEN:	Now Peter – it's all right, isn't it?
PETER:	Is it?
ROGER:	But what else is the problem? *(To Maureen)* I mean you *can* have children if you want them ... can't you?
MAUREEN:	Of course he can, if he would just learn to relax and to ...
PETER:	Maureen! Will you shut up! Do you know what you're saying? Listen to the bloody question – he asked about *you* not me.
MAUREEN:	But Peter, *I* can ...
ROGER:	You can. You mean that Peter ...
PETER:	All right! Terrific! Let the whole, curious, interfering family in on it. You can. Great – you never stop trying, do you! Did you all hear that. Maureen can have children. I can't. The cat's out of the bag.
RITA:	The cat?
PETER:	Yes, the bloody cat – all your bloody cats. Why didn't *you* have children? Let's all be honest. What was wrong with you ... or your husband?
ROGER:	Now just a moment, Peter – there's absolutely no need ...
PETER:	You! We all know why you can't. I'm asking her. *(To Rita)* Well, why didn't you have children?
RITA:	I don't see why you have to shout at me.
PETER:	I'll ask you quietly then: why didn't you have children? Tell the family. We are all ready to help. We're all just dying to help. Tell us ...
SUZY:	I don't think, Peter, we ought to ...
RITA:	*(Softly)* I'm not well, Roger. Will you get me some water?
ROGER:	*(Jumping up)* Yes, of course, Rita ...
MAUREEN:	*(Jumping up)* I need some too – after that mad outburst. Peter, you really ought to ...
PETER:	Why are you leaving all of a sudden? Are you after him now? He's not going to be much use to you, you know. What's going to happen out there? And after him, who will it be? One of the twelve cats?
MAUREEN:	Peter! Peter, you promised not to mention that sort of thing.

RITA: Joe, will you pass my handbag, please – my tablets.

ROGER: *(Who has paused)* I'll get the water.

MAUREEN: No, you sit down, Roger – I'll get enough for all of us ...

PETER: Bloody Gunga Din now. First, Jezebel the man chaser; now Gunga Din the water carrier ...

MAUREEN: Stop it, Peter.

PETER: You want me to stop now – convenient – just when we come to your *little* problem.

MAUREEN: I'm getting the water ... *(Leaves)*

JOE: Will I get out your tablets, Rita?

RITA: Thank you, Joe – you're a good boy. Where's the water?

ROGER: Maureen is getting it.

          (Silence as Maureen returns with the water. Rita takes tablet)

SUZY: Okay people, settle down – we've got nothing to worry about. We've had some reaction to our unmaskings and this is good. The session is going well – very well. Now we can try to calmly and helpfully, sort it all out. You okay, Rita?

RITA: Yes, thank you. I don't like people shouting at me. I get turns, you know.

SUZY: Right. Peter, do you want to say something at this point in time?

          (Silence as Peter sulks)

SUZY: Roger?

ROGER: Yes, well I think that we, inadvertently, did a disservice to Peter.

JOE: I agree.

PETER: Christ!

SUZY: Yes we did, Roger. That's so true.

ROGER: We touched on a sensitive nerve – but not in the right way. Peter felt exposed, felt alienated and beyond our understanding. And he reacted. In Oslo, we often discovered that with a little help, this alienation can be ...

RITA: If it will help, I'll answer Peter's question.

SUZY: Fine Rita – that's a positive and mature reaction to a here-and-now situation. Are you with us, Peter? *(Silence)* Okay, go ahead, Rita.

RITA: When we married, I thought of how many children we would have. Two boys, I thought, and one girl – the boys just like their father: quiet, sensitive and understanding

53

	– the girl, smiling and shy. We talked about it many times. I remember on our honeymoon – we took a cruise from Southampton to Malta – we would stand at the ship's rail, watching the surf, and talk of our dreams. My husband loved children and it was a great blow to us to realise that we could never have any. But we learned to accept this and it brought us even closer together. We never had our two boys, or our girl, but we had each other.
MAUREEN:	*(Gently)* How long is your husband dead, Rita?
RITA:	My husband died three years ago – savaged by dogs. That beautiful, gentle, quiet man who had so much to give to the world was savaged by dogs. I miss him so much.
ROGER:	Did you ever form – or try to form – another relationship after he ... died?
RITA:	That would have been impossible, Roger. We didn't have our children but that didn't matter. Nobody – no man could ever have replaced him.
PETER:	Not all wives are so devoted.
MAUREEN:	*(Gently)* Don't say that, Peter.
PETER:	Why not? It's true, isn't it. It's honest ...
MAUREEN:	Peter, I know what you're thinking and you know that it's not true.
PETER:	Isn't it? Then what about Marcus Dalton or Tony what's-his-name or ...
MAUREEN:	Peter, don't ...
PETER:	Tell them about Marcus Dalton, Maureen. Tell them about the famous drive in his new car and the meals you had with him and your see-through dress and your hair all done up for him and ... and ... and the magazine he gave you with all the instructions ...
MAUREEN:	Peter please, you're only ...
PETER:	He did give you the magazine, didn't he? Was that how you were both going to do it? Was it?
MAUREEN:	Peter!
RITA:	We never had any children, but we were so close ...
MAUREEN:	You've explained all that, Rita. He just won't see reason.
PETER:	What reason?
MAUREEN:	*(Quietly to all)* This Marcus Dalton was his business part-

	ner – architect – who one day took me for a drive in his new BMW ...
PETER:	All his great talk and his education and the dinners he had.
MAUREEN:	... And Peter simply refused to come along ...
PETER:	... Come along! Did you want me to sit there and watch the two of you?
MAUREEN:	You don't believe that Peter. Not really ...
PETER:	But I do! I do believe it!
MAUREEN:	You know that there was nothing between Marcus Dalton and I. Nor anyone else. You know that – I've told you ...
PETER:	Can you swear to it? In front of everyone? Can you?
ROGER:	Oh Peter – really now ...
PETER:	Well can you? Ah. Can you?
MAUREEN:	Yes!
PETER:	Right. Go on, swear to it. Let me hear you – in front of everyone ...
SUZY:	Look Peter, I wonder if we could discuss this ...
PETER:	Discuss nothing – let me hear her swear. *(Silence)* See? What did I say? Now you have the two sides. Now you understand.
MAUREEN:	I swear it! I swear that there was nothing between Marcus Dalton – or anyone else – and I. I swear it. Now.
RITA:	That is lovely. Just like the marriage vows of my dear husband.
SUZY:	Peter? Do you want to say something?
ROGER:	I think you honestly ought to acknowledge ...
SUZY:	It's vital for the session that we ...
PETER:	*(Quietly)* Maureen. Do you really swear to that?
MAUREEN:	Yes Peter, of course. Why did you have to do this?
PETER:	It ... it was because of ... of what they said to me ... the children and ...
MAUREEN:	You heard how Rita and her husband felt. I feel the same. I told you that.
PETER:	Yes, it was what they said ... I'm sorry ... I ...
SUZY:	Well, that's sorted out. Everything's AOK.
MAUREEN:	*(To Peter)* Look love, why don't we go to the room for a while and ... talk ...
PETER:	No no, we can't just go and ...

MAUREEN: Come on now, come on ...

PETER: I don't think we're supposed to leave ...

SUZY: Sure you are, Peter. This is our world – this is the only here-and-now. You can do as you please.

MAUREEN: Now come on, love ...

PETER: *(Rising)* I don't think we ought to in front ...

MAUREEN: Come on. Don't worry.

SUZY: Go ahead people. Fine. *(Peter and Maureen leave)*

RITA: *(Sobbing)* I'm sorry. It reminds me of how my husband used to ...

SUZY: That's okay, Rita – it's a great emotional release for all of us.

ROGER: *Amantium irae amoris integratio est.*

RITA: Pardon?

ROGER: Ah 'lovers' quarrels are the renewal of love' – a quotation by Terence of Rome.

JOE: Homer of Greece.

ROGER: Homer? No Terence, the Roman dramatist. Died 150BC.

JOE: Homer, the Greek poet. Died 850BC.

ROGER: No, you're mistaken, Joe.

JOE: Yes, I'm not, Roger.

SUZY: Hey, what the hell, boys – we've all seen a deep-rooted problem solved through our understanding. Doesn't that make us all feel good? And Rita, your honesty made it all possible. Do you know that?

RITA: Do you think so?

SUZY: Sure, Rita.

ROGER: It's true, Rita – you did.

RITA: Oh, do you really think so? Let's celebrate. *(Takes a paper bag from her handbag)* Let's have sweets. Here Joe, have a Liquorice Allsort.

JOE: Oh thank you.

RITA: Suzy, have a sugary one. They're nice.

SUZY: Well, I shouldn't – but why the hell not.

ROGER: Yes, be a devil. *(Also takes one)* Thank you Rita.

RITA: Take two, if you wish, Roger.

ROGER: No no, sufficient for the day and all that.

RITA: I'll have a three-tier one. Oh, I wish my husband were here now.

SUZY: He's here, Rita. In your heart, he's here.

RITA: Yes, perhaps he is.
SUZY: He is, Rita – he's here.
ROGER: Yes, he is.
          (Silence)
JOE: Rita, did it take the ship long to get to Malta in those days?
RITA: Malta? Sorry Joe, what did you say?
SUZY: Joe was wondering how long it took your honeymoon ship to get to Malta.
RITA: Oh, the ship. Well now, Joe, that was a long time ago. I don't really remember. My memory is not good, you know.
ROGER: Of course, we understand.
RITA: But it was a long voyage, I remember that ... A long, beautiful voyage. *(Pause)* Sitting on the deck during the day, holding my husband's hand. And he in his whites – he looked so splendid. I remember how tall he was – he was tall and elegant. And the boy who brought us drinks – yes, I remember him. A young, Italian lad – he would always bow and call me 'your lady'. He was a lovely boy – he'd say 'Would your lady like some tea now?' or 'Is your lady comfortable?' My husband used to be so proud. He was never jealous. Never.
SUZY: You remember quite a lot, Rita. Hey, bet you can even remember the name of the ship.
RITA: The name? Oh the name ... yes ... eh, no. I'm afraid I can't. Perhaps ... oh ... my husband could remember. He had a wonderful memory.
SUZY: I'm sure he had.
ROGER: May I be permitted ... may I ... I would like to give a here-and-now reaction to Rita's recollection.
RITA: A what?
ROGER: A family reaction. We used to do this in Oslo.
SUZY: Oh sure, Roger. A here-and-now reaction, family.
ROGER: Well, I find it interesting that Rita, in recapturing these beautiful moments, has never mentioned her husband's name. And I wonder does anyone feel that there is, perhaps, a subconscious desire in this to preserve an intimate memory?
RITA: Oh no ... did I say? ... didn't I tell you ...?

SUZY:	Sure you did. You said his name was ... Andrew?
RITA:	Yes, that is ... that was ... I ...
ROGER:	No surely, wasn't Andrew one of the names we were trying to remember for your cats?
SUZY:	Right on, Roger. That is correct. So many names ...
RITA:	*(Upset)* Yes, Andrew ... no, my husband's name was ... Tom. Tom was his name. A nice name. Tom.
ROGER:	That is unbelievable, Rita.
RITA:	Unbelievable? Why do you ...? It is *not* unbelievable ...
ROGER:	No – that was just my friend's name at school. Do you remember? I told you about him. Tom.
SUZY:	It was indeed. Tom.
RITA:	Yes, Tom was my husband's name. Yes, I remember thinking of my husband when you spoke of your friend. *(Laughter from room)*
SUZY:	Hey listen – really making it up in the there now.
RITA:	Yes, Tom was his name. Tom. He loved Malta.
ROGER:	It wasn't called Malta then, of course. Or was it?
SUZY:	Sure it was. It was always called Malta.
ROGER:	Even before the war?
SUZY:	Sure. Wasn't it Rita?
RITA:	Wasn't it what? I'm sorry ...
ROGER:	Malta. It wasn't called Malta when you were there, was it?
RITA:	Oh no ... it was ...
SUZY:	I can't think of what it was called ...
RITA:	Would you like another sweet? A two-tier one?
SUZY:	Not for me, Rita.
ROGER:	No, thank you, Rita.
JOE:	Thank you. *(Takes one)*
ROGER:	Ah, it was Persia I was thinking of.
SUZY:	Persia?
ROGER:	That became Iran. Yes, Valetta is Malta's capital – Valetta, Rita?
RITA:	*(Weakly)* We had a Persian cat, you know. That was Andrew. I remember now.
SUZY:	*(Laughing)* How could you confuse Malta with Persia, Roger?
ROGER:	Oh, white heat perhaps. Sunshine. I don't know. I'd like to see Malta. Is it nice, Rita?

	(More laughter from room)
RITA:	*(Fingering her ring)* It's nice to hear that. Do you like laughter, Suzy?
SUZY:	Yeah, like music, I always say.
ROGER:	Malta is nice, then, yes?
RITA:	Yes, my husband could always remember. He was always travelling ... always going away ... going away ...
SUZY:	*(Pause)* I've noticed your rings, Rita. They're beautiful.
RITA:	*(Relieved)* Oh yes – this one was given to me by my brother. It's sapphire.
SUZY:	Ah, you're a Virgo?
RITA:	No no ... yes ... I ... what did you say?
SUZY:	Virgo – your birthstone. August/September.
RITA:	Oh yes, I was born in August.
SUZY:	Then you're a Virgo.
RITA:	Oh, I see.
SUZY:	And this is your wedding ring?
RITA:	Oh yes. My husband put this on my finger *(Pulls ring from finger)* when we ... would you like to see it?
SUZY:	Sure – but I guess it's been so long on your finger that you cannot remove it now, can you?
RITA:	*(Puts ring back)* No no, I can't – it's been so long..
JOE:	*(Stammering again)* May I gi ... give a here-and-now re ... reaction ... ?
SUZY:	Sorry Joe?
ROGER:	Joe is quickly learning the *modus operandi* of our Group. He has a here-and-now reaction for us.
SUZY:	Oh great. Sure Joe. What is it?
JOE:	I th ... think from your questions that you do not believe that Rita was ever in Malta.
RITA:	But I was. *(Upset)* I was. After we married, my husband took me ...
ROGER:	Yes, of course. Joe I think you are greatly ...
JOE:	... and that you do ... don't really believe that she was even ma ... married ... married.
RITA:	I was, I was ... I cannot remember because it was so long, but I was ...
SUZY:	Easy Rita, easy. That's just Joe's here-and-now.
RITA:	Just because I cannot remember doesn't mean ... he was always travelling ... but he came back ... he ...

59

ROGER:	Of course, of course.
RITA:	He promised to take me to Malta and he ... did ...
SUZY:	Sure Rita, take it easy ...
ROGER:	*(To Joe)* Look what you've done now!
JOE:	I just have a here-and-now reaction to your questions ...
ROGER:	For Heaven's sake, our questions were just communication ... conversation..
JOE:	Inquisition!
ROGER:	What? No, no, communication. Rita said she was married and we ...
RITA:	I was married to Tom. I told the truth. I was, I ... *(Laughter from room)* ... said I was ... my husband was ... *(More laughter)* ... Who is laughing? Why are they laughing?
SUZY:	Relax Rita, that's just Peter and Maureen ...
ROGER:	It's perfectly all right now ...
RITA:	Well, I don't know ... I can't remember ... Can I have a glass of water ... I take turns when I'm upset, you know ...
SUZY:	Fine. Roger, get some water, will you?
JOE:	No, I'll get it.
ROGER:	I'll get it, blast you.
JOE:	*(Runs to Contemplation Room door)* I'm getting it.
SUZY:	Now Rita, you're fine ...
JOE:	*(Knocking at door)* Open up.
MAUREEN:	*(From inside)* What is it, Joe?
JOE:	I want a glass of water.
PETER:	*(From inside)* For God's sake!
ROGER:	You're perfectly all right now, Rita.
JOE:	*(Door is opened. Joe enters)* Just want water. *(Door is closed)*
RITA:	Can I have a glass of water?
SUZY:	Joe is getting it, okay?
RITA:	I was married ... I was ...
SUZY:	Of course Rita – do you have a tablet? *(Joe returns with water)* Ah here's the water.
ROGER:	*(To Joe)* Give it to me.
JOE:	No, I'll do it.
ROGER:	Give it to me. *(Takes glass)* Now Rita, sip this slowly.
SUZY:	There. Do you have a tablet?
JOE:	She has them in her bag ...
RITA:	No, I'll rest now. I just want to rest. Just to rest.
ROGER:	Yes, do *(Stands. To Joe)* You and your talk. What an idiot

	thing to do!
JOE:	It was just a here-and-no ... now ...
ROGER:	You didn't have to say it.
JOE:	You ... you ... you were saying it.
ROGER:	I certainly was not.
JOE:	I was only being ho ... honest in a here-and-now ...
SUZY:	*(Standing. They move away from Rita)* Okay, drop it. She's resting now. She's fine.
Maureen:	*(From room)* Peter – no! *(Laughter)*
PETER:	Yabadaba-dooooooooo. *(Laughter)*
ROGER:	There was absolutely no need for this to happen.
JOE:	You me ... mean she could have told us?
ROGER:	Told us what?
JOE:	That she wasn't marr ... married.
ROGER:	Who said she wasn't for Heaven's sake?
SUZY:	Okay, okay, leave it at that – we've got another problem now.
ROGER:	What other problem?
SUZY:	*(Sternly)* I'll give it to you straight. Peter and Maureen's reconciliation is based on Rita's story – right?
ROGER:	That's true yes.
SUZY:	Now I don't want this new experience to be spoiled – I don't want this whole session ruined by someone deciding to blow this whole thing about Rita wide open. I want no reference to it whatsoever.
ROGER:	Look Suzy, do you think it would be better if we just said there was a misunderstanding ... ?
SUZY:	*(Mock good humour)* Roger, just relax ...
JOE:	... relate, communicate ...
SUZY:	*(Angrily)* Shut up, Joe! *(Sternly to Roger)* What I want done, I want done for the sake of the session. This session is going to work and I'm not going to have ...
JOE:	Sh ... Sh ... shouldn't we be honest?
ROGER:	Well, that's rich coming from you, I must say.
SUZY:	Drop it please! I'm going to ask for a show of hands right now. Do we skip what was said about Rita?
	(Movements heard from Contemplation Room)
MAUREEN:	*(From room)* Peter, come on ... come on ...
PETER:	*(From room)* Yabadaba-dooooooooo.
MAUREEN:	Peter! *(Laughter)* That's enough – we're going out now.

(Laughter)

SUZY: Look, we've got to decide now – we can't upset the whole session by ...

JOE: Do ... do ... does Rita have a vote?

SUZY: *(Angrily)* Right! If I don't get an immediate show of hands, I'm phoning Paddy. *(Joe shoots up his hand)* That's one. Roger, I want it unanimous.

ROGER: *(Slowly)* I'm not so sure, but ... *(he raises his hand)* Oh well ...

SUZY: *(Now more relaxed)* Okay folks, we can all hang loose now. *(They will return to their places)* Everything's going to be okay – I'll make this session work. Just relax ...

JOE: ... relate, communicate. Relax, relate, communicate ...

ROGER: Do you have to act the parrot at a time like this?
(Peter and Maureen enter. They are holding hands)

SUZY: Hey, you're looking good, people.

MAUREEN: We are good – aren't we, love?

PETER: Oh, we're good all right. I'm good, you're good, we're good. Yabadaba-doooooooooo.

MAUREEN: Oh dear, poor Rita – is she all right?

JOE: She took a turn.

SUZY: No, she didn't. She's fine. She's resting. We had a long conversation. Didn't we, Roger?

ROGER: Yes, we had indeed.

MAUREEN: Poor dear – it is late, of course. We wanted her to tell us more about her husband and Malta, didn't we, Peter?

PETER: That's true, love – we did.

SUZY: Well, she's sleeping now – hey, did you two talk it all out?

MAUREEN: Oh, we talked all right ...

PETER: ... occasionally and a bit of yabada-dooooooo.

MAUREEN: *(Lightly)* Please Peter – yes, we had a great talk – our first real discussion for years – talked abut our lives and *(to Peter)* dare I mention, Marcus Dalton?

PETER: You may dare – just once.

SUZY: That's really good. So you've sorted it out, eh?

MAUREEN: We have. And we owe it all to Rita – and to you all, of course.

ROGER: Yes, we understand.

PETER: If she hadn't told us about her life, we would ...

SUZY: Great. See, the group is working, working ... and while

	you were out, we were solving problems, making decisions, becoming aware ...
JOE:	... taking votes ...
ROGER:	Joe! We were just talking ...
MAUREEN:	Oh, you must tell us what you discussed ...
RITA:	*(Awake)* I miss him so much ... Tom. I miss Tom ...
ROGER:	That's all right, Rita.
PETER:	Ah, she's awake.
MAUREEN:	Rita? Hello – we wanted to ask you ...
RITA:	*(Sipping water)* I had a sleep ...
SUZY:	Okay, we'll leave that for a while – eh, would anyone like to discuss anything else ...? Like to discuss anything? Anything? Roger?
JOE:	I want to talk about something.
ROGER:	Now Joe, don't forget ... what we said.
PETER:	You said? What was said?
SUZY:	Okay, okay, fine. Right Joe, what do you want to talk about?
MAUREEN:	Something happy?
JOE:	*(Happily)* Yes, a funny story.
SUZY:	Great, Joe – go ahead.
JOE:	Not about Malta.
ROGER:	For heaven's sake, Joe ...
JOE:	I said *not* about Malta. It's funny.
ROGER:	Your ideas of fun are ...
RITA:	I like funny stories. I like laughter.
SUZY:	Like music – eh Rita?
RITA:	Yes, I like music. *(Searches her handbag)*
JOE:	It's about my father ...
MAUREEN:	Oh lovely. Come on, Joe – you never mentioned your father before.
JOE:	Well, when I was young, my father ...
RITA:	*(Still searching handbag)* Wait, I've got to see if my tablets are ... oh, here they are.
SUZY:	You okay, Rita?
RITA:	Yes, I just like to know where they are.
JOE:	Well, when I was young, my father was a porter in a railway station and he had a little cap and a worsted uniform and he used to tear tickets in half – or clip them – and wave a green flag ...

ROGER: We know what porters do!

MAUREEN: Shhhhhh.

JOE: And he had a little silver whistle with a pea in it and he used to blow it when the train was ready to leave ...

ROGER: *(Quietly, anxiously to Suzy)* Is this about his train again?

JOE: It's a *funny* story.

SUZY: Go ahead, Joe – it's okay, Roger.

JOE: Anyway, one day – it was summer – the train had to take on five churns of milk and my father was helping the guard of the train with the churns, when they suddenly noticed this boy standing on the platform saying good-bye to an older boy who was on the train. So, for a laugh – my father could be very funny – they decided to be as slow as they could – so that they would leave the two boys talking. So they kept rolling the five churns onto the train and taking them off again and the boys were still there – and then my father said that he'd like to check the wheels on the train – and that took more time – and then they took the five churns off again – and then, suddenly, a police car stopped outside the station and these two policemen got out – and there was a tall, grey-haired man with them. And my father knew that man – he was the headmaster of the local boarding school. And the policemen and the man ran along the platform and grabbed the boy who was saying goodbye and took him away ...

PETER: Hey, that sounds very like Roger's story of saying good-bye to his ... his ... his friend.

MAUREEN: To Tom, you mean.

JOE: No, no, it's different – Roger didn't say anything about the police ...

RITA: And what happened, Joe?

JOE: Well the boy on the train was shouting and screaming at them. So my father blew the whistle with the little pea in it, waved his green flag and the train went off.
(Silence)

MAUREEN: Is that all?

JOE: Yes.

MAUREEN: But why was he screaming?

JOE: What?

PETER: Why did the police come?

JOE: Oh. Well, my father knew the headmaster and he said that they were taking the boy back to school to finish his studies.

PETER: Oh.

JOE: Yes, my father heard later that he became a priest and went on the missions to the Philippines.

MAUREEN: And what about the other boy?

JOE: Ah. He was expelled from school – but the funny part of the story was my father putting the churns on the train and taking them off again.

(Silence)

PETER: *(Weakly)* Yes, that's funny all right.

SUZY: Right, fine. Eh, you liked your father, Joe?

JOE: I used to see him at the station – blowing his whistle and waving his flag.

SUZY: But you liked him?

JOE: The boy's name was Roger, I think.

RITA: Roger? That's the same as ... *(indicates Roger)*

SUZY: Which boy? The one who became a *padre*?

JOE: A priest. No, I don't know what his name was.

SUZY: The other one?

JOE: He was ...

RITA: Roger? Why, that's a coincidence. My husband's name was Tom, and Tom's friend was Roger, and Roger is the name of ...

JOE: *(Quietly)* I heard that he was expelled from school because, one night, there was a younger boy who ...

ROGER: That's it! I knew it! I've been waiting for this ... this is another of this fool's lies, his insinuations ... I know what you're saying.

SUZY: Roger!

ROGER: He's an incurable liar, that bastard. He's ...

RITA: Roger, you're shouting.

SUZY: Hold it, Roger.

MAUREEN: What is this all about?

JOE: I don't know – I just heard my father saying that ...

ROGER: Don't you know? It's about me, isn't it? I'm supposed to be ...

SUZY: Roger, calm down. Let the family analyse this ...

ROGER:	Don't analyse me with those lies.
JOE:	You're hypersensitive, Roger.
RITA:	Why is everybody shouting?
ROGER:	Hypersensitive!
JOE:	Yes, like what Peter said about the boy he knew with the mole on his leg who would never take off his trousers when he went swimming ...
MAUREEN:	*(Laughing)* What boy, Peter? I didn't know you knew a boy with a mole on his leg ...
PETER:	I don't know any boy! Get a grip on yourself!
ROGER:	That was me, for heaven's sake.
RITA:	Do you have a mole on your leg, Roger?
SUZY:	No, it's Roger's story, Rita. You remember: nobody noticed the boy's mole, but *he* was so sensitive about it.
JOE:	Roger is hypersensitive – like that boy.
ROGER:	Hypersensitive be damned! It's this bastard who ...
JOE:	No no no – why is everyone getting *(Stammering again)* ex ... ex ... excited? It was a fu ... funny story ...
ROGER:	And that's another one of your tricks – that stammer ...
MAUREEN:	Now Roger, that's not fair.
SUZY:	Yes, I don't think it's right to ...
ROGER:	It's all games, lies, tricks ...
JOE:	Not lies ... my father told me that the train ...
ROGER:	Was that like the train you threw your cat under?
RITA:	His cat? What cat?
MAUREEN:	*(Laughing)* Look, I really think we ought to ...
ROGER:	Yes cats. You upset everyone with that and then you tried to make Rita say that she didn't marry her husband and go to Malta ...
PETER:	What? Didn't she say..?
ROGER:	... well, you're not going to make me admit ...
PETER:	But didn't she go to Malta? You told us that ... Rita, you told Maureen and I that ...
ROGER:	To hell with Maureen and you! He did the same to you and were it not for Rita, your marriage would be in bits.
PETER:	Our marriage is not in bits!
ROGER:	And if you now believe that his father ever worked on the trains ...
JOE:	He ne ... never worked on the trains ...
ROGER:	Ah see? The story is changed again. So he never worked

	on the trains..
JOE:	He was a porter in the station. I said that.
ROGER:	Just listen to him.
JOE:	I merely said that my fa ... father told me that Roger was expelled from school..
ROGER:	*(Shouting at Joe)* Shut up! Don't start that again.
SUZY:	Okay okay okay. That's enough folks.
RITA:	I don't like all this shouting ... my husband never shouted ... he was gentle ...
SUZY:	Yeah okay. Now everything is fine. Let's get it all sorted out. We've had an exchange – now let's pause, hang loose and relax. Let's think of the session, okay? Okay Joe – you have said that ...
ROGER:	Yes, let's have some more lies ...
SUZY:	Roger, there's probably a good explanation ...
ROGER:	Oh there is – he's a liar, that's the explanation. He has an eternal string of lies ... come on, then let's have some more. Come on ...
JOE:	I do ... don't think that anyone was really being hon ... honest about ...
ROGER:	Hear that? *We're* not being honest! What about your cat?
JOE:	I had a cat ...
ROGER:	And a dream?
JOE:	And a dream and a father ...
ROGER:	Who worked as a porter ... and what else? A black toothbrush?
JOE:	Yes, there's a black toothbrush ... in my pocket ...
ROGER:	What else?
JOE:	There's a van that I drive ...
ROGER:	A van yes – come on – what else?
JOE:	A sister who died ...
ROGER:	Yes, what else ...?
JOE:	A bomb in my bag ...
ROGER:	Yes, what else ...
JOE:	A dream I had when I ...
ROGER:	Dream. Yes. Come on, come on, come on ...
PETER:	For God's sake, calm down.
ROGER:	Calm down? You had difficulty calming down when he said that your wife was over-sexed ...
MAUREEN:	*(Laughing)* Ha. Who said that?

PETER:	Don't you dare speak about my wife like that.
SUZY:	Hold it, hold it, folks.
ROGER:	Well, it's true.
PETER:	It's not bloody-well true.
SUZY:	*(Shouting)* I said hold it right there! *(Silence. Rita sobs)*
SUZY:	Okay now, quietly. I just want to know one thing. What did you just say, Joe?
JOE:	Me?
SUZY:	Yes, you. About your bag.
JOE:	My bag?
SUZY:	Come on. Joe. Did you mean what you said?
PETER:	What did he say?
ROGER:	Rubbish – he's been talking rubbish for so long ...
SUZY:	Quiet Roger. Joe, did you not say that there was a bomb in your bag?
JOE:	Oh that. Yes.
RITA:	A bomb?
SUZY:	Shhh, Rita. Is it true, Joe?
ROGER:	How can you expect an honest answer to that?
SUZY:	Joe, I'm asking you – is it true?
JOE:	Yes, it's in my bag.
PETER:	A bomb! What bag? Where's his bag?
MAUREEN:	Quiet, Peter.
PETER:	Don't quiet me.
SUZY:	Is it in your bag outside the door, Joe?
JOE:	Yes.
PETER:	For Christ's sake – is he serious?
ROGER:	Is he stammering – that's the question. He only stammers when he's serious. Will you never learn.
JOE:	*(Stammering)* It's outside the do ...do ... door.
ROGER:	There now – he's done it for us. All panic now.
PETER:	Oh my God – my merciful God! Maureen?
MAUREEN:	Stop that, Peter – be quiet.
SUZY:	*(Calmly)* And this bomb, Joe – when will it explode?
JOE:	I don't know. I just set the timer. I don't know.
PETER:	Jesus Christ, Maureen – he set the timer ... the bomb ...
MAUREEN:	Stop it, Peter!
PETER:	Stop it? You stop it – stop stopping me!
MAUREEN:	Suzy, what can we do now?
ROGER:	Oh for Heaven's sake, he has you all going again. He'll

	apologise in a minute.
SUZY:	No Roger, this is no joke anymore. I'm going to phone Paddy and have the police called ... check this out ... we got to do this thing ...
ROGER:	Well, do that by all means, if you wish, but ...
JOE:	Phone's not working.
PETER:	What! What do you mean? Are we ... all locked in here with a bloody bomb ...
SUZY:	The phone's okay, Peter – just relax. *(Takes the key from her shirt, goes to the phone)*
ROGER:	Just relax, everyone – nothing to worry about Rita – just prepare to laugh at Joe's latest joke.
RITA:	*(Rising)* I'd like to go home now ...
ROGER:	It's only a game, Rita. Lie back there. Rest.
RITA:	You were shouting, Roger.
PETER:	If it's true about this bomb, I'll kill that bastard ...
MAUREEN:	*(Stiffly)* If it's true, darling, you won't need to.
PETER:	What the hell are you talking about?
ROGER:	She's right, Peter. And if it isn't true – which it's not – I'll help you to kill him anyway.
SUZY:	*(Tapping phone)* Hello, hello, Jeez, that's strange. Hello ...
PETER:	What's wrong? Is it not working?
SUZY:	No, it's okay. Just getting a line here. Hello ...
PETER:	*(Jumping up)* Here, let me try.
MAUREEN:	*(Laughing)* Ah good – Peter will fix it.
SUZY:	It's okay, Peter ...
PETER:	*(Taking phone)* Jesus Christ – it's dead.
ROGER:	Dead? What do you mean?
RITA:	*(Getting up)* Let me try – I have a phone that sometimes ...
ROGER:	Rita, sit down – I'll see to it. You must rest.
PETER:	Not a bloody sound.
ROGER:	Sit down Rita. It'll come back.
PETER:	*(Finding torn flex)* Jesus, Look! Look! The phone's wrecked. He's wrecked the phone.
MAUREEN:	*(Rising)* Now Peter, come here. We'll ask Joe.
SUZY:	*(Shouting to Joe)* Did you do this? Did you? Answer me – did you?
ROGER:	What? Did he break ...?
PETER:	*(Laughing wildly)* Jesus, he's going to kill us all – he really is. We're all dead ...

SUZY:	Did you? Answer! Did you?
JOE:	Yessss. *(Jumps up and runs towards the Contemplation Room. Is held by Roger)*
ROGER:	Just a moment *(Joe falls to the ground)*
PETER:	*(Rushes over and kicks Joe)* Bastard! Killer!
MAUREEN:	Stop that ... Peter! Stop that!
RITA:	*(Banging on entrance door)* Help! Oh, Tom, Tom, Tom ...
PETER:	*(Catching Joe by throat)* You bastard – I'm going to make sure you're the first to go ...
ROGER:	Is there a bomb? Let him talk. Is there?
MAUREEN:	*(Pulling at Peter)* No Peter, no. Let him be ...
ROGER:	Is there a bomb?
PETER:	I'll choke the truth out of him.
SUZY:	Hold it! Hold it, I said.
MAUREEN:	He can't breathe, he can't breathe. Let him go.
ROGER:	Let him tell us – is there a bomb? *(Catches Joe by hair. Peter is pulled back by Maureen)*
JOE:	You're all supposed to be controlled – but you're frightened – just like her, just like her.
PETER:	*(Kicks at Joe)* Is there a bomb?
MAUREEN:	Coward! Let him be, coward!
PETER:	Don't call me that, you.
RITA:	Tom, Tom, Tom, Tom.
PETER:	Will you stop that shouting.
SUZY:	Yeah, shut-up Rita – the place is soundproof ...
PETER:	*(Kicks at Joe again)* Bastard!
JOE:	My sister was frightened like you all ... she was frightened, every night, after you'd finished with her ...
ROGER:	Don't start that again – is there a bomb?
SUZY:	Hold it! Come on, Joe – tell us abut your sister.
ROGER:	Fairy tale time again. What about the bomb? What about the phone?
SUZY:	If you two don't stop, we'll get nothing out of him. What happened to her, Joe?
JOE:	All your in-depth analysis, your here-and-now debates – you did that to her. You all remind me of her now – frightened. All your prying ...
PETER:	Jesus, what's he talking about?
SUZY:	Go on Joe.
JOE:	And then you left her, went back to your comfortable

70

	bungalows, purged of all your imaginary hang-ups, back to your ex-group conventions, your cocktail parties ... but *she* was quiet when she got home ...
RITA:	I can't hear him. What did he say?
ROGER:	He's talking rubbish again.
SUZY:	Easy. Yes Joe?
JOE:	She was like all of you – frightened, mad, waiting, silent ... after you all had left her ...
MAUREEN:	I didn't know your sister, Joe?
ROGER:	There's no sister ...
SUZY:	Shut-up, all of you. Joe, listen carefully. Nobody knew your sister, not anyone here ... we never did anything ...
ROGER:	The little bastard hasn't got a sister at all ...
JOE:	Yes, you're right – but I had one – until she climbed down the railway embankment, waited for the train to come and threw herself under the wheels ... she escaped, smeared along the tracks for a hundred yards ...
MAUREEN:	No, Joe, No ...
SUZY:	We never knew her ...
JOE:	Just different faces in a different time ... but it was all of you ... her body along the railway line ...
ROGER:	Wait a minute! That's the story of his cat ... his dream ... not his sister ...
PETER:	He's mad ... he's mad ...
ROGER:	It's his cat he's talking about ... his dream ...
JOE:	See if it's a dream – when the bomb explodes!
ROGER:	*(Gripping him by the hair again)* Is there ... ?
PETER:	*(Kicking out at Joe)* Blast you to hell ...
MAUREEN:	*(Pulling at Peter)* Peter, for God's sake, let him go ...
PETER:	Shut up – get away from me..
ROGER:	Is there? Is there a bomb?
MAUREEN:	Coward! Coward! Coward! *(As Peter grabs Joe)*
PETER:	Coward am I! I suppose Marcus Dalton was a better man.
RITA:	*(Banging on door)* Help me, Tom. Help me.
MAUREEN:	Yes, Marcus Dalton was a better man. At least he was a man. He was a man.
PETER:	Ah, it's all out now.
MAUREEN:	Yes it is. He was a real man – not a coward!
RITA:	Tom, Tom, Tom ...

71

SUZY:	Get away from that door, Rita – the bags are outside..
RITA:	*(Runs to the Contemplation Room)* Help me ... !
	(Peter and Roger kneel beside Joe, hitting him)
SUZY:	Stop it, for Christ's sake, stop it! Get to the Contemplation Room! Quick!

PETER & ROGER: Liar! Bastard! Liar, tell us, tell us ...

MAUREEN: Cowards, cowards – Half-men, you're only half-men!
(Joe goes limp, falls over. Silence as all watch)

MAUREEN: Oh, my God ... Oh, my God ... Oh, my God ... Oh, my God ...

LIGHTS OUT.
END OF SCENE ONE, ACT TWO.

ACT TWO

Scene Two

Joe is lying on the floor. Stage is otherwise deserted. Hold for fifteen seconds. Contemplation Room door is unlocked and slowly opened. Maureen looks out.

MAUREEN: He doesn't seem to have moved at all. Do you think he's dead?

PETER: Will you close that bloody door. If the bomb goes off now, we'll all be blown to ...

MAUREEN: Suzy, don't you think we ought to see if he's dead?

SUZY: *(Looking out)* Well, yeah, okay. Roger, would you like to see if he's ... all right?

ROGER: Me? You don't seriously expect me to walk out into a damn explosion ...

SUZY: Peter, will you go?

PETER: I'm bloody sure I won't.

MAUREEN: Well, I didn't really expect a hero like you to go out anyway.

PETER: You go – you're so interested in him.

MAUREEN: I *will* go.

PETER: And close the bloody door after you.

SUZY: Okay, Okay, Maureen. I'll go.

ROGER: *(Appearing)* No, stay, I'll look at him.

MAUREEN: Is he breathing? See if he's breathing.

ROGER: I can't see from here. *(Moves nearer)* Joe?

PETER: Will someone close that door.

ROGER: No, no – don't close it!

SUZY: It's okay, Roger – we won't.

ROGER: Joe? Can you hear me? Joe?

JOE: *(Not moving)* Roger, what's going to happen?

ROGER: He's alive. He's just spoken.

MAUREEN: Thank God. What did he say?

PETER: He asked for you, I suppose.

MAUREEN: Shut-up. What did he say, Roger?

ROGER: Joe, are you all right? *(Silence)* He just asked what is

73

	going to happen. That's all.
PETER:	Jesus, that's great. He's the one who planted the bloody bomb.
JOE:	*(Quietly)* No bomb ... no bomb. All a game ... all a game, Roger. For the session. A here-and-now.
SUZY:	What did he say, Roger?
ROGER:	He says there's no bomb. *(To Joe)* Are you sure? How can we be sure?
MAUREEN:	*(Laughs)* There's no bomb. It was all fun. Great.
JOE:	No bomb ... all games ... just games ... you shouldn't have hit me ... I'm dying ... I'm dying ...
SUZY:	What did he say, Roger?
ROGER:	Nothing ... he's all right. *(To Joe)* Now come on, Joe, – is there a bomb or not?
JOE:	No bomb. Nothing ... I want to go to the jacks, Roger. I'm sick ...
SUZY:	How's he, Roger?
ROGER:	There's no bomb – he thinks he's going to be sick.
SUZY:	*(Coming across to Joe)* Is that right, Joe?
JOE:	Yes, I'm going to be sick ...
SUZY:	No, about the bomb ...
JOE:	No bomb ... all games ... session games ... therapy ... I'm sorry ... I want to go to the jacks ...
ROGER:	He means the loo. I think he's telling the truth.
MAUREEN:	Joe? Are you all right?
SUZY:	He's just been out for a few hours, that's all.
ROGER:	Try to stand ... slowly.
PETER:	*(Appears)* Florence bleedin' Nightingale attends to the virile troops!
MAUREEN:	*(To Peter)* I'll hold your virile little hand in a minute. *(To Joe)* How do you feel, Joe?
RITA:	*(Appears)* What's happening?
JOE:	I want to be sick ... the jacks ...
SUZY:	Okay, let him ... Roger, help him walk.
	(Roger and Joe cross to Contemplation Room)
RITA:	Did it explode? Is he dead?
PETER:	Yes, it exploded. We're all in bloody hell – they're taking him up to Heaven!
SUZY:	It's all right, Rita – there's no bomb – you just sit down.
JOE:	*(Shaking off Roger)* It's all right. I can find it myself.

74

ROGER: Are you sure, Joe? *(Joe enters the Contemplation Room)*

SUZY: Okay, okay folks – just relax now. Sit down, everyone. Sit down.

ROGER: *(To Rita)* How do you feel?

RITA: I took a turn. Would you like a sweet?

ROGER: Oh, no thanks.

SUZY: Not for me, Rita.

RITA: I'll keep them for later. *(Pause)* You were shouting, Roger. I remember.

ROGER: Yes, I don't know ... why. I mean ... I was hitting him. I never, never did that to anyone.

SUZY: So why don't we explore that now? Let's not waste the session. Let's use it to explore our true feeling about ...

PETER: Marcus Dalton, for example.

SUZY: The session can still work for each of us, Peter.

JOE: *(From room)* Hey, family. *(The Contemplation Room door is noisily and ominously bolted by Joe. The group reacts to this)*

SUZY: Joe? you okay, Joe?

JOE: Yes. In my bag, outside the door, there's a bomb.

PETER: What? Jesus Christ!

SUZY: *(Jumping up)* What did you say, Joe?

JOE: You're all sitting beside it – it's due to go off. In my bag ... *(All run to the Contemplation Room)*

RITA: Open up, open up – open this door at once.

ROGER: Rita, don't scream ... don't.

MAUREEN: No don't, Rita.

PETER: *(Kicking door)* I'll kill you, I'll kill you ...

ROGER/PETER: Open the door, open the door ...

            (Entrance door is opened. Paddy stands looking. He is carrying some bags)

PADDY: Good morning. *(Pauses, looking at the panic)* Good morning. *(Shouts)* I said Good Morning!
            (All turn. Silence)

PADDY: Here we are – the sun is up, the streets are aired, it's time for all of us to ...

SUZY: *(Controlled)* Paddy, look Paddy now – is that Joe's bag you've got there?

PADDY: This one – yes.

PETER: Get to hell out of here with it!

ROGER: There's a bomb ...

SUZY: Take it easy, for God's sake ...

PADDY: Bomb? What bomb?

RITA: I want to go now. (*Moves towards door*)

ROGER: (*Holds her*) Don't move, Rita.

SUZY: Now listen, Paddy – turn and chuck that bag down the
           stairs ...

PADDY: Chuck it where?

MAUREEN: Just throw it away, Paddy.

PETER: There's a bloody time-bomb in that bag!

SUZY: Chuck it away, Paddy ... Now.

PADDY: There's nothing in this bag ...

ROGER: There is ...

MAUREEN: Throw it away ...

PADDY: There's not ...

PETER: Are we going to stand here while he argues ...

SUZY: There's a bomb in it – throw it away ...

PADDY: There's nothing in it – I looked.

SUZY: You looked?

PADDY: I ... eh ... I supervised all the bags ... (*Begins to open bag*)

PETER: No ... Jesus ... No ...

SUZY: Paddy ... don't ...

PADDY: (*Empties bag onto floor*) See? Nothing. Towel, soap, a
           book, a clock, a spanner, a toilet roll, box of envelopes,
           bunch of keys ...
           (*Silence*)

SUZY: You're not supposed to do that ... to look into bags.

PADDY: Well, I sometimes just ... eh ... supervise the bags, as they
           say ... (*Door of Contemplation Room opens. Joe appears*) ...
           Ah, hello, sunshine – hey, what happened to you?

PETER: (*Rushes over to hit Joe*) Bastard ... Liar ...

PADDY: Hey, what's going on?

SUZY: Okay, take it easy ...

ROGER: (*Holding Peter*) Leave him be, now. Peter, leave him.

SUZY: Now, Joe, what's all this about?

JOE: What?

ROGER: (*Resigned*) He asks 'what'!

SUZY: You know what. Why did you do this? Why did you try
           to ruin my session?

JOE: My bag! (*Sees contents on floor*) What happened to my
           bag?

76

PADDY:	I ... eh ... they were looking for a bomb, sunshine.
JOE:	A bomb?
PADDY:	They said that there was a bomb ... in your bag.
SUZY:	That's enough, Paddy. Pick up these things.
PADDY:	Yes, Miss Bernstein.
JOE:	There's no bomb in my bag.
PADDY:	I know sunshine, I told them that.
SUZY:	That's enough, Paddy – do as I say.
	(Paddy gathers Joe's belongings into the bag)
	Look people, we have a lot to talk about here ... so let's relax for a while ...
PETER:	Relax my arse – I've had enough of this – therapy ...
JOE:	*(Quietly)* Ha – that's good all right.
SUZY:	Peter, look people – if we don't sort this out, then it's all wasted, all worthless, we'll have achieved nothing ... I'll ... we've ... ..We'll have failed in our session.
PETER:	That's right, I'm going. Come on, Maureen.
MAUREEN:	Don't talk to me like that.
RITA:	I'd like to go home too.
ROGER:	Would you really?
RITA:	Yes.
ROGER:	If you like I can drive you to ...
RITA:	If my husband were alive he'd drive me – he was a quiet, gentle person ...
ROGER:	I understand.
RITA:	He used to drive me everywhere. He was gentle ...
ROGER:	I understand.
SUZY:	Hold it, hold it – we can sort this through communication – just relax ...
JOE:	... relate, communicate *(To Paddy)* That's what we do here.
PADDY:	Yeah – signs of it! *(Picks up bags)*
ROGER:	I ... I'll get your coat from Paddy.
SUZY:	Look, will you all just sit down for Christ's sake ...
PADDY:	*(To Roger)* Here you are sir. *(Holds out hand for a tip)* It's been a pleasure attending to you ...
ROGER:	Thank you – goodbye, Suzy. Are you ready, Rita?
RITA:	Yes, Roger. *(To Paddy)* Thank you, young man.
PADDY:	It's been a pleasure bringing you your meals and sweeping up after you. *(Waits for a tip)*

RITA: Yes, thank you. Have I my tablets? Yes. Goodbye to you all now. *(To herself)* I didn't like the shouting – I take turns, you know ... *(Leaves with Roger)*

PETER: Now, are you coming or not?

PADDY: Ah, your bag, sir – it's been a pleasure attending ...

SUZY: Will you knock it off, Paddy!

PADDY: I was just giving him his bag ...

SUZY: Peter. We've had problems, but if we scatter, the group will have failed – and I'm determined not to allow that to happen ...

PETER: Are you coming?

MAUREEN: No!

PETER: Will I send Marcus Dalton over for you then?

MAUREEN: Don't bother.

PETER: *(Indicates Joe)* Him, is it? Mother of God, is it him?

MAUREEN: Wouldn't you like to know.

PETER: Well, *I'm* going ... now ...

MAUREEN: Well go! Now!

PETER: Blast you, Maureen – I'm not going to wait for long, mind you ... I'm not waiting for long..

PADDY: Goodbye sir, it's been a pleasure ... *(Peter leaves)*

SUZY: Paddy – sweep! Sweep out the Contemplation Room and shut-up!

PADDY: Yes, Miss Berstein. I'll leave your bag here, sunshine. *(Goes to Contemplation Room)*

JOE: Grand. Thanks Paddy.

SUZY: Okay, okay – go. The group session is closed – failed. You've all failed. *(Picks up clip)* You're all supposed to sign this, you know. What the hell. Forget it. *(Writes on clip. Silence)*

MAUREEN: You're priceless Joe – do you know that? You're a dream-maker – a nightmare-maker. *(Laughs)*

JOE: Yes – that's life or something.

MAUREEN: No you really are. I don't know why you did those things.

JOE: Don't you?

SUZY: The group is closed – we're locking up. *(She exits to Contemplation Room)*

MAUREEN: Yes. Well, it was different ... a bit different.

JOE: Was it?

MAUREEN: Oh it was. *(Pause)* Well, I must go now, Joe.

JOE: To Peter?

MAUREEN: Of course – why not? Why wouldn't I?

JOE: Yes. He builds good bungalows.

MAUREEN: Don't belittle it, Joe – he does. He works hard.

JOE: You have a good home ...

MAUREEN: ... house.

JOE: Split-level.

MAUREEN: It's something.

JOE: Split-level something ... .

MAUREEN: Well, mustn't keep Peter waiting.

JOE: ... or he'll be up again.

MAUREEN: Huh, there's a joke there somewhere.

JOE: Yes.

MAUREEN: So, goodbye Joe.

JOE: Goodbye.

SUZY *(off)*: Paddy, you better lock that door downstairs.

MAUREEN: Locks on doors, bricks on windows, Peter waiting ...
(Leaves. Joe picks up his bag. Paddy comes from room)

PADDY: Ah, sunshine – still here?

JOE: Just going ...

PADDY: *(Quietly)* Jaysus, I warned you, didn't I?
Said you weren't the type, didn't I?

JOE: You did.

PADDY: What the hell did they do to you?

JOE: Oh nothing. Curiosity – nearly killed the cat. Remember, you said that.

PADDY: Don't remind me, sunshine. I'll tell you one thing though – if it's not being too personal. Your little stammer. It's gone, isn't it?

JOE: Oh yes. It is.

PADDY: Noticed that as soon as I came in. You're talking grand now.

SUZY: *(Emerging)* Paddy? Paddy, I thought I told you to lock the door and to ...

PADDY: Yes, Miss Bernstein – I'm going. Good luck now, sunshine.

JOE: Goodbye Paddy. *(Paddy leaves)*

SUZY: All right sir – you can go now. We're closed.

JOE: Yes. It went quite well, didn't it?

SUZY:	Will you please get out.
JOE:	A real in-depth analysis – true colours showing all around.
SUZY:	Are you going?
JOE:	Yes. *(Turns to leave)* Oh, about the honesty thing.
SUZY:	Yes?
JOE:	Texaleto.
SUZY:	Texaleto? What the hell are you talking about? Don't play games with me.
JOE:	Where you came from. You told Roger. Remember?
SUZY:	Look, the place is closed, so will you please get out and close the door.
JOE:	It's not in Utah.
SUZY:	What isn't?
JOE:	Texaleto. It's in Arizona. Texaleto Arizona. It's worth knowing because I told Paddy. He knows now. Arizona. *(Joe leaves. Suzy waits. She rushes to the door)*
SUZY:	Hey, I'll tell you about that. *(Silence)* Hey, I said I'd tell you. *(Silence)* Hey, what about the phone you broke? What about that? *(Silence)* And the way you wrecked the session. What about that? *(Returns from door. Pauses thoughtfully. Flings clip-board across the room)* God-damn freaks! Who could run a therapy session with them!!

BLACKOUT

ALL IN FAVOUR SAID NO!

All in Favour Said No! was first presented at the Abbey Theatre, Dublin on 2 April 1981 with the following cast:

GILBERT DONNELLY	Bill Foley
MISS TEMPLE	Kathleen Barrington
CHRISTY METCALF	Kevin McHugh
DAVE	Stephen Brennan
LIAM	Nicholas Grennell
SALLY	Martina Stanley
UNA	Bríd Ní Neachtain
JOAN	Fiona MacAnna
DEE KAVANAGH	Máire O'Neill
MIKE REYNOLDS	Emmet Bergin
EDDIE MALONE	Tom Hickey
RONNIE PARTRIDGE	Godfrey Quigley

DIRECTOR	Patrick Laffan
DESIGNER	Wendy Shea
LIGHTING	Tony Wakefield

FOR MARGARET AND DES

ACT ONE

Scene One

Scene: The offices of Donnycarney Metal Works. The back wall has large observation windows. These look down on the factory floor, far beyond and below. Through these windows, we see the upper section of high machine belts onto wheels. (If not possible in production, the illusion of these belts will suffice).

Entrance to the office is from the factory floor – that is, up a metal staircase at S/R (unseen), across a metal passageway which runs along beyond the observation windows and then through the door in the back wall at stage left. Hence, anyone approaching is first seen (through the windows) from S/R to S/L. The playing area is really only a section of a total office complex. This complex continues off stage right.

A switchboard is against the side-wall at stage left. It has a built-in public address microphone. Its chair faces the wall. Next – from S/L – is Liam's desk, next – more upstage – is Gilbert's desk. Next, at the back wall, is Sally's desk. Then we come to Dee Kavanagh's desk.

Dee's desk guards the entrance door of a box-office which has been crudely built into the complex's open-plan design. This is Mike Reynolds' private office. It is only partly visible, built against the back wall and continuing off-stage right. It does not reach fully down stage – thereby leaving a corridor off stage right to the remainder of the complex. We can see into Mike Reynolds' office through a window on the corridor-side of it. This window has an open venetian blind.

The whole complex is normally comfortable and quiet. But, whenever the entrance door is opened, the noises of the factory machines are clearly heard.

It is morning. The machine belts can be seen working. The office, however, is empty. Now we notice Gilbert Donnelly coming along the passageway. In his early sixties, he is easy-going, gentlemanly and pleasant. He carries a little suitcase, wears an expensive overcoat. He also wears a soft hat. He enters, closes the door and pauses. Looks towards Mike Reynolds' office. Goes over, looks in through the window.

GILBERT: *(Satisfied, announces)* Last night I lay a-sleeping there
                came a dream so fair. *(Goes to his desk, taking off his coat. Sings with great feeling)* Last night I lay a-sleep-

ing, there came a dream so fair; I stood in old Jerusalem beside the Temple there. *(Pauses. Settles his hat firmly on his head)* Aye. *(Takes a rose from his suitcase. Examines it. Announces)* Roses are shining in Picardy, in the hush of the silvery dew. *(Puts the rose into his button-hole. Sings with great feeling)* Roses are shining in Picardy, in the hush of the silvery dew; roses are flowering in Picardy but there's never a rose like you. *(Pauses. Puzzled by the note for 'Rose'. Sings)* ... but there's never a *rose* like you. *(Pauses. Quietly)* Never mind. *(Sings)* And the roses will die with the summertime and our roads may be far apart, but there's one rose that dies not in Picardy ... *(Christy Metcalf enters. He is forty-five. He looks undernourished and uncared-for. He speaks quietly, nervously)*

GILBERT:	*(Now seated at his desk)* Ah, good morning to you, Christy.
CHRISTY:	Morning Gilbert. *(Looks towards Reynolds' office)* His nibs in yet?
GILBERT:	Not a sign, Christy. We are alone. *(Sings)* One alone to be my own; I alone to know her caresses.
CHRISTY:	*(More relaxed)* Good. *(Awkwardly again)* Nip in the air this morning.
GILBERT:	And rain to come. Registers in the voice, I find – makes the tone just that bit off. Aye.
CHRISTY:	Oh, the singing? Yes.
GILBERT:	*And* the trumpet, I daresay?
CHRISTY:	The trumpet? Oh – no, it's the coronet I play. Actually, I don't play it much at all now – just teach the boys in the club.
GILBERT:	And off-key, were they? The boys?
CHRISTY:	No, I ... I never noticed. But ... but they're only learners.
GILBERT:	Very obvious in our rehearsals last night – even Rose Marie herself was off-key. Knew right away it was the damp weather. *(Laughs)* Knew why some of the Mounties were a bit slow in getting their man. Aye.
CHRISTY:	Yes? *(Nervous again)* Anything after, about Liam, was there?
GILBERT:	What's that, Christy?

CHRISTY: *(Awkwardly)* You know – anything after about Liam refusing to do the machine call-off in the factory? Any more about it after?

GILBERT: *(Lightly)* Oh that? No, nothing there. No word what-so-ever. All quiet on the Western Front.

CHRISTY: *(Concerned)* That could be serious, Gilbert. As ... as the union representative, I haven't been officially in-formed of any change in clerical duties and ... and ... if Liam is given an instruction again to go to the fac-tory and refuses, you ... you ... never know what Reynolds *(Indicates Reynolds' office)* might do.

GILBERT: Aye. Well, yesterday came and went, as they say.

CHRISTY: Yes, but yesterday's different, Gilbert. Reynolds mightn't *take* a second refusal and ... and he's had time to think ...

GILBERT: *(Pleasantly)* Time and the river, Christy – time and the river.

CHRISTY: The ... the members have already taken a lot in this place, Gilbert. If they ask for action, I might have to ... I *will* ... eh ... act. And if the members want action then it's up to me ... *(Sees Liam and Dave approaching)* Well, you'll let me know if anything ...?

GILBERT: Oh rest assured. Christy, rest assured.

CHRISTY: Thanks, Gilbert.

(Christy goes quickly along the corridor to his office. Liam opens the door, is about to enter – but Dave has turned and is leaning over the passageway rail. Both Dave and Liam are about twenty-three. Dave is good-looking and extro-vert. Liam is less assured. Both are well-dressed in suits. Dave carries the morning paper)

DAVE: *(Shouting down to the factory floor below)* Hey Una! Uuuuuuun-a! Hey, who was yer man at the bus stop with you last night? *(Pause)* Who? Dracula? *(Laughs)* Hey, you must be mixin' him up with Liam here. He's the one with the fangs!

LIAM: *(Suddenly offended)* Ah God, Dave – not over the whole factory floor!

DAVE: *(Shouts down)* Mess off yourself! *(Takes a plastic rat out of his pocket. Shouts)* I'll get my rat after you. Suas do guna, Una. I'm tellin' ya! *(Turns. Comes into the office.*

85

Normal accent now. To Liam) That Una is all right.

LIAM: Good morning, Gilbert – Mr Reynolds in yet?

GILBERT: Good morning to you, boys. Mr Reynolds is a non-starter so far. *(Quotes to himself)* And the roses will die in the summertime.

DAVE: *(To Liam)* Remember the night I brought her back to the flat?

LIAM: Una? Oh yes.

DAVE: Thought she was going to rape me, that night. She reminds me of the English one we met in Salthill – the blonde one – Susan. Una reminds me of her. Well-stacked ... and givey.

(Liam is now at his desk. Dave sits on the edge of it)

LIAM: *(Pre-occupied)* Yeah. *(Seriously)* About the other thing, Dave – you really think I should stick by my decision not to ...

DAVE: *(With sudden authority)* Liam – Liam, you go down to the factory and read off those numbers *once* – and you've set the precedent. That's all they want. They'll come along then and say 'it's been done before, why can't it be done again?' And we'll have lost more ground.

LIAM: Yeah. *(Proudly)* When I refused yesterday, I thought that Reynolds was going to ...

DAVE: Look. *(Indicates Sally's desk)* Your woman, Sally, is *still* temporary: a job left unfilled; a man out of the Invoice Department three weeks ago and never replaced; there's new work being designated without anyone asking questions ...

LIAM: And they moved *you* out of this office.

DAVE: *(Suddenly defensive)* Oh well, hold on now – that was a *transfer*. No – asking a clerk to go onto the factory floor is totally different.

LIAM: Yeah. *(Pause)* Anyway, I don't think Reynolds will ask me again today. *(Pause)* But if he does ...

DAVE: If he does, there's one thing for sure – Christy will back you ...

LIAM: I know that.

DAVE: ... the office staff – overall – will back you and the factory floor will back you. *(Quietly. indicates Gilbert)* I

86

	don't know about 'The Singing Hat' here ...
LIAM:	Ah well – he's my *boss* and ...
DAVE:	He's in the union too!
GILBERT:	*(Sings with great feeling)* But there's one rose that dies not in Picardy, that's the rose that I keep in my heart. Aye.
	(During this, we see Miss Temple approach the door. She now enters. She is about fifty. She carries a white stick and a long, hessian bag. She wears dark glasses. She walks confidently to the switchboard)
MISS TEMPLE:	Good morning, Gilbert. Very seasonal this morning.
GILBERT:	Good morning to you, Miss Temple – yes, it *is* seasonal but there's rain to come: registers in the voice.
MISS TEMPLE:	Oh, did your rehearsal go well last night?
GILBERT:	Aye – no. The Mounties were all off-key – even Rose Marie herself emitted the occasional strangled note.
MISS TEMPLE:	*(Pause)* Do you know that strangulation is the most common form of murder, Gilbert?
GILBERT:	Aye – is it really?
MISS TEMPLE:	Yes, it was on the radio last night. The BBC.
DAVE:	*(Very sarcastic)* Did you listen to 98FM last night, Miss Temple?
	(Miss Temple sits at the switchboard. She takes a large screwdriver from her hessian bag. Feeling across the board she unscrews the safety-catch. She then organises her headphones)
MISS TEMPLE:	No, but I was just telling Mr Donnelly that I heard that strangulation is the most common form of murder. It's also one of the slowest.
DAVE:	*(Quietly)* That so?
MISS TEMPLE:	*(Quietly)* Oh, they said that strangulation can be very slow indeed.
	(Sally arrives. She is twenty – she is a temp. Unsure of herself, eager to please)
SALLY:	Good morning, Mr Donnelly.
GILBERT:	Ah, Sally – Sally, pride of our alley.
SALLY:	Hi Liam – I'm afraid every bus for Donnycarney was absolutely packed this morning. I suppose I *could* have dashed back and asked Daddy to drive me – but I'm afraid *that* would have taken *hours*.

LIAM:	*(Friendly)* You're okay – Reynolds is not in yet.
MISS TEMPLE:	Very seasonal this morning, Sally.
SALLY:	Oh hello, Miss Temple – yes, I'm afraid it is.
DAVE:	*(Sarcastic)* Sally, is there anything you're *not* afraid of?
SALLY:	*(Pause)* I'm afraid I don't know, Dave. *(Embarrassed laugh)* Except, perhaps, being left here temporary forever *(Intimately to Liam)* or becoming a nurse.
DAVE:	*(Not amused)* Yeah. *(Quietly to Liam)* Hope you never think of bringing that one back to the flat. *(Goes off along the corridor to his office)* Nurse! – you wouldn't have the patients.
SALLY:	*(Working)* Oh, very funny.
MISS TEMPLE:	*(Answering a call)* Donnycarney Metal Works, good morning. *(Pause)* Will you hold please for Mr Reynolds? *(Phone rings and will continue ringing in Reynolds' office)* It's ringing.
GILBERT:	*(Sings quietly)* The bells are ringing, for me and my gal.
LIAM:	*(Anxiously)* Miss Temple, he's not in yet. Mr Reynolds isn't in. *(Miss Temple, with headphones, answering calls, doesn't hear)* Miss Temple? *(To Sally)* If Mike Reynolds comes in and hears his phone ringing, he'll hit the roof.
SALLY:	*(Gushing)* Oh. *(To Gilbert)* Mr Donnelly, I'm afraid someone should answer Mr Reynolds' phone.
LIAM:	*(Anxiously)* Miss Temple? Miss Temple?
MISS TEMPLE:	*(Answering a call)* Donnycarney Metal Works, good morning.
SALLY:	*(Stands)* Mr Donnelly, if you like I'll see ...
GILBERT:	What? No no, Sally – my responsibility.
LIAM:	*(To Gilbert)* You could take it at the switchboard – it'd be quicker.
GILBERT:	Aye, at source, eh Liam? *(Turns to the switch)*
MISS TEMPLE:	*(Still answering the second call)* Yes, will you hold please for Gilbert Donnelly. *(The telephone on Gilbert's desk now rings)* It's ringing.
GILBERT:	*(To Miss Temple, indicating Reynolds' call)* I'll take that here, my dear.
MISS TEMPLE:	*(Assuming he refers to his call)* Very well, Gilbert. *(Into*

88

	phone) I'm putting you through to Mr Donnelly now. Thank you.
	(The phone stops ringing on Gilbert's desk. Miss Temple gives Gilbert the hand-set. The phone in Mike Reynolds' office continues to ring. Miss Temple is now busily answering and transferring calls)
GILBERT:	*(Into phone)* Mr Reynolds is not available ... *(Shouts)* Albert! *(Has call transferred to his desk)* Albert White! You old son-of-a-gun! What?
LIAM:	*(Panic)* He's taken the wrong call! If Reynolds comes in ...
SALLY:	*(To Liam)* Then maybe you should answer that one. *(Indicates Reynolds' office)*
GILBERT:	*(To all)* It's Albert White in from Guernsey. *(Into phone)* Aye, still here, Albert.
LIAM:	*(Shouts)* Gilbert! *(Goes to Reynolds' office. Stops. To Sally)* No, I better not go in ...
MISS TEMPLE:	*(Into PA)* Phone call for Mr Reynolds please. Mr Reynolds.
LIAM:	Oh God – Miss Temple, don't ... *(Goes towards Reynolds' office again. Stops)* No – if he saw me in there ... *(Goes towards Gilbert)* Gilbert? Gilbert?
GILBERT:	*(Into phone)* Yes, indeed we are: *Rose Marie*.
LIAM:	*(See Reynolds coming)* Oh Christ – here's Reynolds! Gilbert!
GILBERT:	*(Sings)* When I'm calling you, ou ou ou, ou ou ou ... *(And continues – Mike Reynolds enters. He is thirty-five, a no-nonsense, highly-efficient manager. Runs to answer his phone)*
LIAM:	*(Moves towards Reynolds' office)* Good morning, Mr Reynolds – I was just about to ...
REYNOLDS:	*(Furiously)* Leave it! Leave it! I'll get it! *(Goes towards his office. The phone stops. He stands)*
GILBERT:	*(Sings)* Will you answer too, ou ou ou, ou ou ou ...
REYNOLDS:	*(Furiously to Liam)* Will you kindly ask Mr Donnelly to step into my office when he has finished his ... performance.
LIAM:	Yes sir.
GILBERT:	*(Into phone)* Be delighted. *(Pause)* Aye, I'll phone Miriam straight away. Aye, we'll get out the wel-

come mat ...

(Reynolds enters his office. Slams the door)

LIAM: My God. Of all the days ...

GILBERT: *(Into phone)* Aye, Albert *(Pause)* The model railway? Six locomotives? Aye, same as myself. *(Pause)* We will indeed. *(Laughs. Pause)* And Ronnie Partridge up a pear tree. Oh, happy days. Tooreloo, Albert, tooreloo. *(Gives hand-set to Miss Temple. To all)* That was Albert White, a lovely baritone ... and his wife, Gladys. Haven't seen Albert for years – oh and do you know where Gladys is from?

MISS TEMPLE: Donnycarney Metal Works – good morning.

LIAM: *(Anxiously)* Gilbert, Mr Reynolds wants to see you in ...

GILBERT: From Guernsey! My Miriam from Jersey and his Gladys from Guernsey. Albert and I met them in London, you know – so best of pals, all of us, ever since. Aye, a lovely baritone and a magnificent model-railway lay-out: four viaducts ... *(Laughs. Sings to the air of 'The Twelve days of Christmas')* Four viaducts, three French locos, two turtle doves and Ronnie Partridge up a pear tree. Used to sing that to old Ronnie in London. Happy days.

LIAM: *(Nervously)* Gilbert, he says you're to ...

SALLY: *(Interested)* Not our Mr Partridge? Our *chairman?*

GILBERT: Oh aye – Ronnie and I *and* Albert were together in London.

LIAM: Gilbert! *(Gets his attention)* Mr ... Mr Reynolds wants to see you in his office ... about the phone ...

GILBERT: *(Moves towards Reynolds' office)* Oh aye, aye. *(Pauses)* Miriam says that Albert's model railway makes mine look like the West Clare Railway ... !

(Dee Kavanagh enters. She is forty-five, mature woman, but glamorous and trendily dressed. Very superior as Mike Reynolds' secretary)

DEE: *(Bad humoured)* The traffic in this city is shit!

GILBERT: Oh, good morning to you, Dee.

(Dee goes to her desk where, when she is not working, she arranges the flowers and glamorises herself)

GILBERT: *(To Liam and Sally)* Aye – The West Clare Railway – but delighted to hear we were doing *Rose Marie.*

90

	(Sings) You belong to me, I belong to you.
DEE:	*(Hard, as Gilbert approaches Reynolds' office)* Yes, Mr Donnelly?
GILBERT:	Aye. I believe Mr Reynolds wishes to speak to me.
DEE:	I'll check *(Presses the intercom)* Hello Mike?
LIAM:	*(To Dee)* I don't think the intercom's been fixed yet, Mrs Kavanagh.
DEE:	Shit! *(Angrily lifts the phone)* Hello? Hello? *(Silence)* Jesus, that woman!
MISS TEMPLE:	*(Into phone)* Calling?
DEE:	Put me through to Mr Reynolds.
MISS TEMPLE:	Hold please. *(The phone rings in Reynolds' office. Is answered immediately)*
DEE:	*(Sweetly)* Good morning, Mike. *(Pauses. Laughs)* Ooooh, did you really? *(Pause)* Yes – I have Mr Donnelly here to see you. *(Pause)* Very well. *(Puts phone down. Angrily to Gilbert)* You can go in.
GILBERT:	*(Pleasantly)* Thank you, Dee. *(Gilbert goes in. We can see him through the window as he talks to Reynolds)*
MISS TEMPLE:	*(Into Phone)* Donnycarney Metal Works, good morning. *(Pause)* His number is ringing. *(We hear a phone ringing off. Then it stops as answered)*
SALLY:	*(Quietly to Liam)* I'm afraid I didn't realise that Mr Donnelly was so chummy with our Mr Partridge.
LIAM:	Yeah – they were in London together.
MISS TEMPLE:	*(Into phone)* Donnycarney Metal Works, good morning.
LIAM:	*(More quietly. Amused)* Miss Temple once told us that one day they all went celebrating and do you know what Mr Partridge had tattooed right across his chest?
SALLY:	What?
MISS TEMPLE:	A great big partridge!
SALLY:	A partridge?
LIAM:	*(Indicates Miss Temple)* Yes. She was going to tell us something about Gilbert too – but then she stopped.
MISS TEMPLE:	*(Into phone)* Hold please. I'll page her.
SALLY:	*(Pause. Amused)* You know – Mr Donnelly sometimes reminds me of my father.
LIAM:	Gilbert does?

SALLY:	Just the way he goes all quiet: that's my father every time I refuse to leave here and take up nursing.
MISS TEMPLE:	*(Into PA)* Call for Jacinta Kelly. Jacinta Kelly to the phone please.
LIAM:	Well, when you're made permanent, he'll have to accept it.
SALLY:	Oh, I'm afraid he won't. He just insists that because my mother was a nurse and my sister is a nurse, that I must be a nurse too. It's infuriating – he just has this mental picture of me nursing.
LIAM:	*(Gently)* Maybe you would be a nice nurse.
SALLY:	*(Annoyed)* I wouldn't. I'd hate it. I hate the very thought of it.
DEE:	*(Loudly)* Sally, did you ever have dinner at the Chateau René?
SALLY:	*(Lost)* No, I, don't think so.
DEE:	Ghastly place. Last night, unpredictable Larry arrived home and said some of his business sods wanted a night out and it had to be the Chateau. Absolutely ghastly food – duckling that looked like it gave itself up and cauliflower that I'd swear was rescued from somebody's dust-bin.
SALLY:	*(Mock horror)* Oh never, Mrs Kavanagh.
DEE:	Larry, of course, wanted to apologise to everyone – even the bloody waiters. Silly sod. *(Christy comes along the corridor. He has paused to peep into Reynolds' office. Goes to Liam)*
DEE:	*(To Sally)* Jesus – I mustn't forget to ring that woman to come over on Thursday. *(Mock intimacy)* Two of his company directors – Larry gets so bloody hysterical about hosting ... I told him that, if he left, who would design their bloody churches and halls for them.
SALLY:	Yes. Exactly.
CHRISTY:	*(Confidentially and nervously)* What's that all about, Liam – Donnelly in there. What's all that?
LIAM:	*(Softly)* Oh, about a phone left ringing, Christy. I don't think it's about ... me.
DEE:	*(Continuing to Sally)* For God's sake, I said to him, don't become all duodenal over a bloody dinner –

	when I have to host for this lot, I said, *(Indicates Reynolds office)* I don't collapse at Ronnie Partridge's feet, do I? Larry's such a bloody whimp sometimes.
CHRISTY:	*(Quietly)* Stupid bitch. *(Softly to Liam)* Well, you know where I am. *(Puts his hand paternally on Liam' shoulder)* You have total support from ... from us all on this one. All right? *(Notices Dee looking. Immediately takes his hand away. Now quickly, nervously)* No matter ... no matter ... no matter how it goes, you have my ... word, Liam complete solidarity. Every one of us. Every worker. All right?
LIAM:	Thanks Christy – but I don't think he'll ask me again.
MISS TEMPLE:	*(Into phone)* Donnycarney Metal Works – good morning.
CHRISTY:	He's pushing, Liam – trying to make a name for himself. We never had this kind of trouble before he arrived in from Shannon ...
MISS TEMPLE:	*(Into phone)* Hold for Mr Metcalf. *(A phone rings off)*
CHRISTY:	That's for me *(As he goes)* Don't forget now.
LIAM:	Yes Christy. And thanks.
	(Christy hurries off along the corridor)
DEE:	*(Continuing to Sally)* When I think of it now, Larry was always a bloody whimp. Before we married, he wouldn't join my tennis club because he didn't want everyone to see his little bony legs. *(Gives Sally some papers. Off-hand)* Oh, file those, will you.
SALLY:	*(Goes to her desk)* Yes, Mrs Kavanagh.
DEE:	*(Continuing to Sally)* And because he damn-well knew that I'd beat the pants off him. *(Pause)* Miserable sod.
	(Reynolds' door opens. Gilbert gloomily enters)
GILBERT:	*(Crosses to his desk. Sings dejectedly)* Lift that bar, tote that bale; you gets a little drunk and you lands in jail.
LIAM:	*(Nervously)* Everything all right, Gilbert?
GILBERT:	What's that, Liam? Oh aye – everything in the garden is rosy ... I must ring Miriam – she'll be delighted to see Albert and Gladys again. Aye – I'll ask her to set up the model railway of Crewe for tonight. Aye.
	(Reynolds suddenly enters. Goes smartly to Sally)
REYNOLDS:	*(Puts papers on her desk. Across to Gilbert)* Mr Donnelly,

	invoices for each of these, in duplicate, endorsed 'repeat', on my desk in ten minutes.
GILBERT:	*(Confused, but recovers)* Aye. What? Oh aye – good girl, Sally. Aye.
REYNOLDS:	*(Moving away. To Sally)* Ten minutes.
DEE:	Mike?
REYNOLDS:	*(More pleasant)* Dee?
DEE:	This bloody intercom is still not fixed.
REYNOLDS:	*(Sharply to Gilbert)* Mr Donnelly, I want that intercom operational this morning. You'll see to that?
GILBERT:	Oh aye. *(Pause)* See to what, Mr Reynolds?
REYNOLDS:	*(Tense pause)* The intercom, Mr Donnelly – I want it repaired and working within the hour. If you can't find the telephone number of the repair people, ask Miss Temple to find it for you.
GILBERT:	Ah, aye, aye I will.
DEE:	Thank you, Mike. Coffee?
REYNOLDS:	*(Going towards office exit door)* Eh, five minutes, Dee. Inside. Make it strong.
	(Reynolds leaves. Through the observation windows, we see him walk briskly to the factory. Gilbert immediately lifts the telephone)
LIAM:	*(Quietly to Sally)* My God – he's like a maniac.
	(Sally is working. Dave enters along the corridor. He carries a file and his newspaper)
DAVE:	*(To Dee)* Last month's returns on exports completed, balanced and awaiting Mr Reynolds' signature. Hand them inside, will I?
DEE:	*(Coldly)* Mr Reynolds has gone down to the factory. You may leave them with me.
DAVE:	Right *(To Liam)* Well?
LIAM:	No – nothing. Nothing about the machines at all.
DAVE:	Great. *(Opens his newspaper)* It's question-time so. Sally, how's your brain-box this morning – you only got one right yesterday. *(Sally works on)*
LIAM:	No – she got the one about Vesuvius.
DAVE:	Vesuvius? We all got the one about Vesuvius! *(Turns out the page)*
MISS TEMPLE:	*(Into phone)* Calling?
GILBERT:	*(Into phone)* Ah Miss Temple – is it 289967417 or 714?

MISS TEMPLE:	714 Gilbert. Will I dial it for you?
DEE:	*(Sharply across to Gilbert)* Tell them I want it fixed now, Mr Donnelly.
GILBERT:	*(Into phone)* Yes, thank, Miss Temple. *(He replaces his phone)*
DAVE:	How about yourself, Liam? *(Laughs)* Going to really get your false teeth into this quiz today, are you?
LIAM:	*(Suddenly upset. Whispers)* Dave – for Christ's sake!
DAVE:	What's up with you? *(Indicates Sally)* She knows about your false teeth, doesn't she?
LIAM:	*(Anxiously)* All right, all right – I'll get two of the three right.
DAVE:	*(Loudly)* Well? Doesn't she?
LIAM:	*(Angrily)* Are you asking the questions? *(The phone rings on Gilbert's desk)*
GILBERT:	*(Into phone)* Gilbert Donnelly speaking.
MISS TEMPLE:	There's your number, Gilbert. It's ringing. *(Dee immediately crosses to Gilbert's desk)*
DEE:	*(Sharply to Gilbert)* This morning! Make sure they get here this morning!
GILBERT:	*(Into phone)* Hello? Hello?
DAVE:	*(Reads from paper)* Now. 'What, in 1953, was achieved by Sherpa Tensing'?
LIAM:	Sherpa Tensing? Oh eh ... ? *(Thinks)*
GILBERT:	*(Into phone)* Oh, pussy-cat – do you know who has just phoned me from the airport this morning?
DEE:	*(Aghast to all)* Sweet God! He's ringing his stupid wife!
GILBERT:	*(Into phone)* Albert White! *And* Gladys!
DEE:	*(To all)* That's his bloody wife – *not* the repair people!
GILBERT:	*(Into phone)* Aye – phoned me *here* ...
DEE:	*(Exasperated. To Sally)* Has that man *ever* performed any worthwhile function in this company?
LIAM:	*(To Dave)* He climbed Mount Everest, didn't he?
DEE:	*(Furiously to Liam)* What are you talking about?
LIAM:	*(Innocently)* Sherpa Tensing – climbed Mount Everest.
DEE:	*(Furiously)* I suppose you think that's funny – but you wait until you're instructed to call-off the numbers on the factory floor! I can tell you that Mike Reynolds has had enough of you and your stupid

	carry-on. You're due for a rude awakening, my boy. *(Goes back to her desk)*
GILBERT:	*(Into phone)* Aye – the record of *Rose Marie* – we'll have it ready.
LIAM:	*(Quietly to Dave)* What did she mean by that?
DAVE:	*(Quietly)* Ignore her. *(Loudly)* I think you're right about Tensing. Did you know that one, Sally?
SALLY:	*(Looking up)* Oh yes.
DAVE:	*(Sourly)* I'm sure you did. Now here's one for you. *(Reads)* 'Who wrote the lament on Keat's death called Ad ... Adonais'?
LIAM:	I think it was Shelley.
MISS TEMPLE:	*(Turning)* Shelley's body was cremated on the beach where he drowned, but his heart wouldn't burn. *(Silence)* Edward Trelowny put his hand into the fire and took it out. *(Pause)* And Mary Shelley kept it in a silk purse and carried it with her wherever she went.
DAVE:	*(Pause)* His heart? She kept his heart in a silk purse?
MISS TEMPLE:	*(Adamantly)* Oh yes. After Napoleon died, they kept his stomach in a silver pepper-pot for a whole year. *(Dee walks off along the corridor to get the coffee)*
DAVE:	*(Quietly)* Oh Jesus.
MISS TEMPLE:	It was all on the BBC last week. *(Pause)* Or was it RTE?
DAVE:	*(Recovers)* I think you're right about Shelley, Liam. We'll see at the end. *(Looks at his paper)* Now, where are we?
GILBERT:	*(Into the phone)* Oh yes, my love – piano accompaniment *would* be a lovely idea.
MISS TEMPLE:	*(Into phone)* Donnycarney Metal Works – good morning.
LIAM:	*(Concerned about Dee. To Dave)* I ... I'd say she heard something, Dave – what she said about the factory floor – about me and Reynolds.
DAVE:	Not at all. Do you think Reynolds tells her anything? *(Laughs)* All Reynolds has her for is to lash her up against the wall in there from time to time. And that keeps *her* happy too – because her poor Larry is ... eh ... a bit weak in that department. Now, here we are – oh, a bit of Greek mythology: *(Reads)* 'Apollo's twin-

	sister, Artemis, loved music yet she was called the Destructress. Why.' *(Looks up)* Why was she called the Destructress?
GILBERT:	*(Into phone)* Aye – might hit a few wrong notes, but I can try. *(Imitates piano-playing across the desk)*
SALLY:	*(Quietly to Liam)* Apollo was the God of Music, wasn't he?
DAVE:	*(Cutting)* This is his twin sister we're talking about – Artemis.
LIAM:	*(Thoughtfully)* Artemis – did she blind people or something.
	(Miss Temple hears this and half-turns, interested)
DAVE:	*(Authoritatively)* I'm not so sure – but I think she was the one who used to fight her enemies by firing deadly arrows. *(Opens another page)* Anyway, we'll see.
MISS TEMPLE:	*(Quietly. Returns to her work)* Deadly arrows.
GILBERT:	*(Into phone)* Yes, pussy-cat, after the music, we'll have the lay-out of Crewe: Aye, three locos on two viaducts with a fiddle yard and a half dog-bone – and an obtuse crossing.
DAVE:	*(Checking the answers)* I had the first one anyway – Everest.
GILBERT:	*(Into phone)* At lunch-time. Right. Tooreloo, my love. *(Puts phone down. To all)* There – a musical evening and the railway lay-out planned for Albert and Gladys. *(Picks up the phone again)* Intercom repair now. *(Dee comes along the corridor with the coffee)*
DEE:	*(To Sally)* I'll be out for those in a moment. *(Goes into Reynolds' office)*
DAVE:	*(Reads)* And I knew about Shelley.
MISS TEMPLE:	*(Into phone)* Calling?
GILBERT:	*(Into phone)* Do you have the number of that telephone repair chap, Miss Temple?
MISS TEMPLE:	289947174 – shall I get them for you, Gilbert?
GILBERT:	*(Dials)* ... One, seven, four. Have them now, my dear. *(Listens. Quotes)* Ah – when I hear your love-call ringing clear.
DEE:	*(Comes from office)* Thank you Sally. *(Takes invoices. Glances at Gilbert. Returns to office)*

DAVE:	*(Reads)* 'Artemis while loving the music of Apollo, killed mercilessly by firing her deadly arrows.' *(To all)* I got that one and strange, only heard about it a while ago. *(Spreads the newspaper on Liam's desk to indicate the answer.*
	Mike Reynolds enters smartly from the passageway. Sees Liam reading the paper. Liam nervously pushes it under his desk)
REYNOLDS:	*(Briskly to Dave)* Returns?
DAVE:	*(Smartly)* Yes sir, listed and balanced – with Mrs Kavanagh for your signature.
REYNOLDS:	*(To Sally)* You finished those accounts?
SALLY:	On your desk, Mr Reynolds.
GILBERT:	Oh, eh, Mr Reynolds?
REYNOLDS:	*(Pauses. Turns)* Mr Donnelly?
GILBERT:	No reply from these repair chaps at all. Perhaps ...
REYNOLDS:	*(Smartly)* Never mind that now. The situation we discussed this morning? It has been finalised Mr Donnelly. You will issue the directive as we agreed.
GILBERT:	Oh aye. Aye. Mr Partridge has been told then, has he?
REYNOLDS:	*(Sharply)* What's that, Mr Donnelly?
GILBERT:	Mr Partridge, our chairman – he has been told then, has he? Informed.
	(Silence. Dee enters from Reynolds' office)
DEE:	Coffee ready, Mike. Inside.
REYNOLDS:	Thank you Dee. *(Sharply to Gilbert)* You will issue that directive, Mr Donnelly and you will then take the action appropriate to the situation. Is that understood?
GILBERT:	Aye. Very Good. We'll do that now *(Quietly sings)* We'll gather lilacs in the spring again.
DEE:	*(As Reynolds goes to his office)* The returns, the invoices, your correspondence are on your desk and I ...
REYNOLDS:	Thank you, Dee. *(He now speaks quietly to Dee)*
GILBERT:	*(Sings)* And walk together down an English lane.
MISS TEMPLE:	*(Into PA)* Will the chief mechanic please return to the loading dock. The chief mechanic to the loading dock. Thank you.
DEE:	*(Quietly to Reynolds)* Absolutely, Mike. *(Reynolds enters*

	his office. Dee sits at her desk)
LIAM:	*(Nervously)* What's all that about, Gilbert? *(Pause)* Is it me?
GILBERT:	Aye. *(Pause)* I'm to instruct you to report to the machine section of the factory floor and to read-off the machine numbers for yesterday's output.
LIAM:	*(Pause)* That's the work of the factory staff, Gilbert – that's not a clerical job – never was.
GILBERT:	Aye. Well. There we are.
LIAM:	When am I to go?
DAVE:	You're not going, are you?
GILBERT:	*(To Liam)* Ah – you're to go now, Liam. Immediately. On the spot, as they say.
DAVE:	*(To Liam)* Do you think they're going to stop there? This is a test case – they want to see how far they can push us.
LIAM:	*(Loudly)* All right! *(Pause. Quietly to Gilbert)* I'm sorry, Gilbert – I'm not going to call-off the machine numbers on the factory floor.
DAVE:	Good man. *(To Gilbert)* Now what?
GILBERT:	Let me see now. Aye *(To Liam)* If you're refusing to go, Liam, I am instructed to issue your suspension from this employment.
DAVE:	I'll get Christy. *(Hurries off along the corridor)*
LIAM:	*(To Gilbert)* I'm to be suspended ... *now* ... if I refuse?
GILBERT:	Aye. That's the way it is. The way the land lies, so to speak.
SALLY:	*(Quietly. To Liam)* Perhaps if you went down for a ...
LIAM:	I'm not going down. *(Pause)* I can't go down.
GILBERT:	*(To Liam)* Tell you what – I'll give Ronnie Partridge a tinkle and see if we can come to some arrangement. *(Picks up his phone – Dee immediately knocks on Reynolds' door and enters)*
MISS TEMPLE:	Calling?
GILBERT:	Aye – if you could contact Ronnie Partridge for me, Miss Temple? Likely over at head office now.
MISS TEMPLE:	Mr Partridge? I'll call you back Gilbert.
	(Reynolds suddenly enters from his office with Dee)
REYNOLDS:	Mr Donnelly, have you implemented my instructions?

GILBERT:	Aye – what's that?
REYNOLDS:	Has he *(Indicates Liam)* been informed of his duties?
GILBERT:	Aye, Mr Reynolds, of course, I've told him and ...
REYNOLDS:	*(To Liam)* Then why are you still here?
LIAM:	Because ... because I refused, sir.
REYNOLDS:	You refused. *(To Gilbert)* You have suspended him for refusing?
GILBERT:	Aye. *(The telephone rings on Gilbert's desk)*
REYNOLDS:	He has been told?
GILBERT:	Aye *(Picks up phone. To Reynolds)* Excuse me. *(Into phone)* Gilbert Donnelly speaking.
MISS TEMPLE:	Your call to Mr Partridge is on the line, Gilbert.
GILBERT:	Ah, thank you, Miss ... *(Reynolds angrily crosses to Gilbert's phone and cuts of the call)*
REYNOLDS:	*(To Gilbert)* Mr Donnelly, I am the manager of this plant. I will not tolerate you using your personal connections with Mr Partridge to undermine my authority ...
GILBERT:	Mr Reynolds ...
	(Christy and Dave enter from the corridor)
REYNOLDS:	*(Loudly to Gilbert)* Mr Donnelly have you carried out my instructions? Has this man refused his duties and, if so, has he been suspended?
	(The phone rings again on Gilbert's desk. Reynolds prevents Gilbert from picking it up)
REYNOLDS:	*(Across to Miss Temple)* Who is that? Miss Temple, who is on this phone?
MISS TEMPLE:	*(Turning slightly)* Mr Partridge was cut off. I have him back on the line now.
REYNOLDS:	*(Angrily lifts Gilbert's phone and replaces it – to cut off)* Don't phone Mr Partridge again, Miss Temple. *(To Gilbert)* Have you or have you not told him that if he doesn't report immediately to the factory floor, he is suspended?
CHRISTY:	Now, just a minute, Mr Reynolds.
REYNOLDS:	*(To Christy)* Ah, Mr Metcalf – I'm glad you're here. This man *(Indicates Liam)* has refused a directive by his superior, Mr Donnelly to perform a duty on the factory floor and his refusal leaves Mr Donnelly with no option but to ...

CHRISTY: *(Nervous but angry)* Mr Reynolds, any re-rostering of duties must first be put to the trade union representative ...

REYNOLDS: *(Turning away)* You're talking gibberish, Mr Metcalf ...

CHRISTY: *(Explodes)* I am not!

REYNOLDS: ... and I'm not here to argue with you.

CHRISTY: *(Furiously)* Yes, I know what you're here for – to promote your own personal career at all costs. Well, this isn't the Shannon Industrial Estate ...

REYNOLDS: Indeed – I had the same trouble in Shannon ...

CHRISTY: *(Furiously)* And what happened there to bring you running up here?

REYNOLDS: *(Triumphantly)* It was due to my success in Shannon, Mr Metcalf – as *you* well know – that Partridges appointed me, not you, to this position.

CHRISTY: *(Nervous recovery)* Too ... too many issues have been rail-roaded here ... why hasn't the temporary staff ...? We're not going to tolerate ...

REYNOLDS: *(Haughtily)* I'll remind you, Mr Metcalf, that this is a business. We are adults here. This is not your club where you reprimand little boys for not playing their trombones properly.

GILBERT: *(Quietly)* Trumpets.

MISS TEMPLE: *(Quietly)* Clarinets?

LIAM: *(Decisively)* Coronets.

CHRISTY: *(Angrily to all)* What the hell ...! *(To Reynolds)* Right. This suspension of our member could lead to ... to industrial action!

DAVE: Exactly.

LIAM: *(Nervously)* Maybe if there was consultation ...

DAVE: *(To Liam)* Shut up.

REYNOLDS: *(To Christy)* Let me remind all of you that this is a branch factory, run at a loss, at present under revision as to its viability ...

CHRISTY: Partridges have used that one before! For years, workers were afraid to ...

REYNOLDS: *(Angrily)* I have no time for debates, Metcalf. If that man refused Mr Donnelly's instructions ...

CHRISTY: He does refuse!

REYNOLDS: Then, as Mr Donnelly rightly says, he is suspended.

101

CHRISTY: Then the members of this union are withdrawing their labour.

REYNOLDS: *(Goes to his office)* Suit yourselves.

CHRISTY: ... and will be supported by the factory floor.

REYNOLDS: We'll see, Mr Metcalf.

CHRISTY: And what about the export ship for this week – that's waiting on the docks. Have you thought of that? That ship could sail *empty* to Hamburg.

REYNOLDS: *(Pause. Turns)* Mr Metcalf, I hope that your members will realise that your sudden militancy is the direct result of your personal lack of promotion with this company. I hope they realise that soon. *(Goes into his office. Slams the door)*

CHRISTY: *(Loudly)* That's an old tactic, Mr Reynolds. *(Silence)*

DAVE: Well, are we on strike?

CHRISTY: *(Nervously)* Yes – yes, we are. I'll inform the ... the other members of the union. *(Pause)* And the other unions too.

DAVE: Great. *(Pause)* So, so what do we do? Go out?

CHRISTY: Yes. We'll go out – later. Well, some of us might stay in. Could be a sit-in. That will have to be ... looked ... to be decided ... as the circumstances are ... examined. *(Emphasises)* But we *have* withdrawn our labour.

LIAM: It's un-official, isn't it, Christy?

CHRISTY: Everything is always un-official at first. Everything begins at this level. But there is no doubt that ... that this action, *our* action will not only be sanctioned by the other union but will be given the ... will be supported by the other unions. I intend to ... to ... to ... to be in ... touch with the ... with ... with them all.

DAVE: *(Not impressed)* Yeah – of course. *(Brightly)* Right – the move has been made anyway.
(Dee picks up her phone)

DEE: *(Tapping)* Hello? Hello? Switchboard?
(Miss Temple turns away from the board and takes out her knitting)

DAVE: *(To Dee)* There's a strike on, Mrs Kavanagh.

DEE: Idiots! *(Slams phone down)* Bloody idiots! *(Goes into Reynolds' office)*

CHRISTY: That's fixed her anyway. The bitch.

LIAM:	*(To Dave)* Maybe if there was consultation ...
CHRISTY:	*(To Liam)* Don't worry, son, you can't be ... you ... we ... we ... you are not *alone* in this.
GILBERT:	*(Sings quietly)* One alone to be my own, I alone to know her caresses.
CHRISTY:	What's that, Gilbert?
GILBERT:	*The Desert Song*, Christy, *The Desert Song*.

FADE OUT
END OF ACT ONE, SCENE ONE

ACT ONE

Scene Two

An hour later. The machine belts are still turning. Sally sits at her desk. Dave, Liam and Gilbert stand looking through the observation windows, down at the factory floor. Miss Temple stands in the middle of the office.

DAVE: *(Angrily)* Ah, Christy is too timid. He's getting nowhere down there – they're not even listening to him, never mind supporting him.

LIAM: *(Looking down)* No – I think he's just explaining.

GILBERT: Isn't that Eddie Malone that Christy is talking to?

DAVE: That's Eddie – the factory shop-steward.

GILBERT: Aye, he had an uncle, Barney Malone, who died down there.

MISS TEMPLE: Barney Malone – yes, he fell into the cutting machines and was slowly fed into the blades. Remember, Gilbert, we could hear his screams up here. They say he died piece by piece.

GILBERT: No no, Miss Temple – they say he died of a heart attack.

MISS TEMPLE: Oh, do they?

DAVE: *(Quietly)* Merciful Jesus.

GILBERT: *(To Miss Temple)* Yes – and that's his nephew: Eddie.

DAVE: *(Looking down to factory)* Ah Christy's getting nowhere with him. Look.

(Dee comes along the corridor. Sits at her desk)

DEE: *(To Sally)* Well, I'm glad to see that someone has a sense of loyalty.

SALLY: I'm afraid it's because I'm temporary that ...

LIAM: *(Looking down)* Christy's laying it down now. Look.

DEE: *(Viciously)* Anyone who'd be part of a union run by Christy Metcalf wants their head examined. To think that he kicked up the most awful row when he did not get that job *(Reynolds' office)* ... *him;* a forty-five year-old bachelor whose only interests are minding his mother and teaching little boys to play the trum-

104

	pet!
LIAM:	*(Looking down)* Ho-ho, there's a move on.
DEE:	*(To Sally)* And now that same idiot is trying to close the place down.
GILBERT:	Ah, he's coming up with him.
DEE:	All idiots. *(To Sally)* I'll use Mike's private phone inside. *(Goes into Reynolds' office)*

GILBERT: Miss Temple, Christy is coming up with Eddie Malone now. We'll see what the word is – where we stand.

DAVE: *(To Liam)* Wouldn't be surprised if Christy has been talked out of it. *(Christy and Eddie Malone appear along the passageway)*

LIAM: *(To Dave)* Talked out of it? He *can't* be.

(Christy and Eddie enter. Eddie Malone is 25/30. Dressed in oily overalls. He exudes self-confidence in union matters and elsewhere)

CHRISTY: Come in, Eddie – this is Dave, Liam, Gilbert Donnelly – all members who have withdrawn labour. *(To all)* This is Eddie Malone – factory floor shop steward.

EDDIE: Morning, gents. *(Indicates Miss Temple. To Christy)* What's the story on her?

CHRISTY: Oh, that's Miss Temple, our telephonist. Also one of our members and also out.

EDDIE: Okay, fair enough. *(To Miss Temple)* You can ignore that phone, lady.

CHRISTY: *(Quickly to Eddie)* She's ... eh ... blind. Can't see.

EDDIE: Oh, okay, fair enough – that'll be taken into consideration re picket duty, et cetera. *(Indicates Sally)* And the story there?

CHRISTY: That's Sally – I told you about – still temporary, non-union ...

EDDIE: ... and therefore working on. Okay, fair enough.

CHRISTY: The rest are in the other offices ... eh ... awaiting developments.

EDDIE: Game ball, Christy. *(Looks around)*

DAVE: Well? What's ... what are we doing?

EDDIE: *(Nonchalantly)* We're out, pal. It's down tools across the factory floor – we're not even taking our tea-break.

DAVE:	Great! *(To Liam)* We did it! We've got them!
LIAM:	*(Relieved)* God – for a while I thought that ...
CHRISTY:	*(To Dave)* Eh, just a moment, Dave – there are a lot ... are some ... elements that make it seem ... that make it inadvisable to take *total* action ...
EDDIE:	Indubiously. And, with your permission, gents, I'll elaborate. *(Indicates Miss Temple)* Someone get that lady a chair before she injures herself.
MISS TEMPLE:	*(Immediately and expertly finding one)* It's quite all right, Mr Malone – I have one.
EDDIE:	*(Looks amazed at Miss Temple. Pause. Now confident again)* Okay, fair enough – the situation in a nutshell. The factory floor downs tools, no sweat – *we* don't want re-rostering *and* we have long-standing grievances that call for consultation – safety matters, et cetera. The clerical staff – yourselves gents – withdraw labour as agreed. So – clerical staff, factory workers out. Okay, fair enough. Now, as usual, there's a ship for Hamburg – five figure contract – so our timing is good. They have to sail that ship full – but not while we're down tools. Okay?
MISS TEMPLE:	*(In same tone)* Fair enough. *(Eddie looks at her)*
LIAM:	Eddie, if the whole thing has stopped, how come the conveyor belts are still conveying loads out to the drivers.
EDDIE:	Fair question. The drivers is – as you may or may not know – members of the second union down there: the Drivers and Handlers Union. *(Sarcastic)* And if any of you, gentlemen, know *anything* about the Drivers and Handlers Union, you'll know that they won't go out – simply because *we're* going out. So, not surprisingly, they will not be supporting us in this stoppage.
DAVE:	But they'll have to support us.
GILBERT:	*(To Eddie)* Aye – they will.
EDDIE:	Gentlemen, they won't – but that suits us.
GILBERT:	*(To Dave)* Aye, it does.
DAVE:	*(Angrily to Gilbert)* How does it?
GILBERT:	*(To Eddie)* Aye – how does it?

EDDIE:	Well, let's look at it this way. The factory closes down completely, what happens? Management can work from another plant – leave us out in a prolonged action, isolate us. But, by us having the drivers working, management can't close *and* they must pay them. And for what? For doing nothing if they have nothing to carry to the ship.
CHRISTY:	And it's this pressure that'll bring management to the table.
DAVE:	So we have them! We really have them!
GILBERT:	Aye, we have *(Quotes. Humorously to all)* We have the sun in the morning and the moon at night. Aye *(Eddie now studies Gilbert)*
LIAM:	And what about the Beltman?
CHRISTY:	*(To all)* The timing, as Eddie said, couldn't be better and sanction from Congress will certainly be ... eh ... forthcoming.
EDDIE:	Oh indubiously. So, any further questions?
MISS TEMPLE:	Yes. Didn't your uncle, Barney Malone, fall into one of the factory machines – wasn't that how he died: cut to pieces in the blades ...?
EDDIE:	*(Shocked)* No, lady, it wasn't. He got a heart attack. The 'oul ticker gave out. *(Recovers. To all)* Anything else.?
LIAM:	What about the Beltman?
CHRISTY:	*(Pause)* The Beltman, Liam, hasn't been approached – mainly because he's non-union – but we don't see any difficulty in his agreeing to turn off the belts.
EDDIE:	*(Confidently)* We needn't worry about the Beltman. He'll be okay.
LIAM:	*(Anxiously)* But if he *doesn't* agree to ...
CHRISTY:	He will.
LIAM:	But if he doesn't, the export orders will continue to be supplied to the drivers who will take them to the ship and ... and ... and the belt *is* stacked up, isn't it? *(To Eddie and Christy)* Isn't it? Aren't the orders for this week's ship all stacked and automatically fed onto the belts? So, so if he doesn't turn it off, the ship will still ...
EDDIE:	A fair point. Just let me assure you that the Beltman

will arrive at this plant at one o'clock today, he will be approached and I am confident that the belts will not be turned on thereafter. Rest assured on that, okay?

CHRISTY: *(To Liam)* Okay?

LIAM: *(Relieved)* I was just anxious that ...

EDDIE: Listen pal – your union has anticipated all these eventualities. *(To all)* Now, what we've decided on, *pro tem*, is a sit-in *and* a picket. The picket will indicate to all unions our dispute; the sit-in further guarantees that management can't shut-up the plant and operate from elsewhere.

DAVE: We'll be drawing up a roster then?

EDDIE: A strictly rota-basis will apply. At this point in time, I suggest the integration of all unions involved in this action – i.e., some of the office staff will sit-in on the factory floor and some of the factory staff will sit-in up here. In this way, gents, I confidently predict immediate sanction by the Industrial Relations Committee of Congress, prompt negotiations and a satisfactory outcome to all our mutual grievances.

DAVE: Great! That's terrific! *(To Liam)* Great!

CHRISTY: *(Thrilled)* I can just see Reynolds' face when he hears what's happening.

DAVE: Oh-ho, he won't forget this.

GILBERT: Aye. *(Sings – from the title song of the musical 'Rose Marie)* No matter what I do I can't forget you.

EDDIE: *(To Gilbert)* What did you say?

MISS TEMPLE: *(Pleasantly sings)* Sometimes I wish that I had never met you.

GILBERT: *(To Miss Temple)* Aye, that's it. *(To Eddie)* That's *Rose Marie*.

EDDIE: *(Looks at Miss Temple)* Oh, I see. *(Pause. Quietly to Christy)* Eh, because of her lamps and that, we won't have Rose Marie *(Indicates Miss Temple)* on picket duty.

CHRISTY: Oh, Miss Temple? Yes, of course. She can sit-in.

EDDIE: Game ball, Christy. *(Loudly)* So now, I think it appropriate if you inform the other offices of our proposals ...

CHRISTY:	Oh, right away – *(To Dave and Liam)* maybe you'd come along to impress upon ...
EDDIE:	Oh indubiously – especially ... *(Indicates Liam)* ... eh ... you as the man-of-the-moment.
LIAM:	Yes, all right.
DAVE:	Right, come on. *(To Christy as they go)* Don't think there'll be any problems now that ... Eddie ... *(Christy, Dave and Liam exit along the corridor. Sally goes into Reynolds' office. Miss Temple sits knitting)*
EDDIE:	*(Hesitates. Now loudly into Miss Temple's ear)* Excuse me, lady – this is Eddie speaking. I just want to assure you that I will keep you informed of all eventualities. Okay?
MISS TEMPLE:	*(In same tone)* Fair enough.
EDDIE:	*(Pause. Now quietly to Gilbert)* Mr Donnelly, a word if you please. To successfully co-ordinate this action, I'd like to be conversant with all personnel involved.
GILBERT:	Oh aye, Eddie. Quite right too. Know thy enemy.
EDDIE:	And thy friends, Mr Donnelly. So *(Looks at Miss Temple)* Perhaps you could tell me something about ... Rose Marie.
GILBERT:	Aye. *(Pause. Puzzled)* Rose Marie? Oh, *my* involvement?
EDDIE:	Well, to be honest, Rose Marie confuses me – so I thought perhaps you'd tell me what the story is there.
GILBERT:	The story? *(Pause)* Well, the story is quite simple really. Let me see. Briefly: Rose Marie came from an Indian family and was raised in ...
EDDIE:	She what? Did you say an Indian family?
GILBERT:	Aye, Indian ...
EDDIE:	Indian ... like the *Apaches?*
GILBERT:	Aye – not really certain of the tribe ... but it was up in Canada. Anyway, she fell in love with a fellow there called Jim Kenyon who was later hunted by the Mounties because they thought he killed a half-breed called ... eh ... Black Eagle.
EDDIE:	*(Slowly turns to look at Miss Temple. Now, back to Gilbert)* Are you serious?
GILBERT:	Oh, no no – don't misunderstand me; *he* didn't kill

	him – he was framed by a chap called Ed Hawley. It was Black Eagle's wife who knifed him.
EDDIE:	Knifed him?! And where did ... our friend (*Indicates Miss Temple*) Rose Marie come into all this?
GILBERT:	Ah – now Rose Marie used to sing in a saloon bar ...
EDDIE:	(*Turns to look at Miss Temple. Then back to Gilbert*) Sing in a saloon bar?
GILBERT:	Aye, that's where she first met Jim Kenyon. Well, she tipped off the Mounties about Black Eagle's wife ... in fact (*Quietly*) to put it bluntly and although it is never said, she offered herself – bodily – to Hawley on condition that he'd tell the Mounties. But (*Quickly*) it never came to that ... never came about that way ... you understand?
EDDIE:	(*Conspiratorily*) Oh, I understand, I understand. That's okay with me, Mr Donnelly, mums the word. (*Looks at Miss Temple*) Jaysas.
GILBERT:	You know the 'Indian Love Call'?
EDDIE:	The what?
GILBERT:	The song 'The Indian Love Call'?
EDDIE:	(*Lost*) Oh yeah, yeah – I think I heard it all right.
GILBERT:	Aye – well, Rose Marie sings that. That's the song she always remembers singing to Jim Kenyon.
	(*Along the passageway, come Una and Joan. Both are eighteen, both are machine workers, dressed in identical overalls and scarves. Joan is smoking*)
EDDIE:	Yeah? (*Nervous Laugh*) You never know, do you? (*Knock on door*) Oh come in. (*Una and Joan enter the office*) Oh, come in, girls, come in. (*To Gilbert*) These will be the representatives of the factory floor for the office sit-in.
GILBERT:	Ah excellent. (*Quotes*) Welcome to our world, won't you come on in.
UNA:	(*Shyly*) Thanks. (*Looks in awe at the office*)
EDDIE:	This is Una, our globe-trotter – and this is Joan (*Pointedly*) who, I understand, is the proud girlfriend of Tim Flynn, *who is the Beltman*.
JOAN:	(*Sourly*) Yeah – so what about it?
EDDIE:	This is Mr Donnelly, girls, with whom you will be sharing the office sit-in.

GILBERT:	*(Shaking hands)* Oh – very pleased. Delighted. Welcome.
UNA:	*(Shyly)* Pleased to meet you.
JOAN:	*(Coldly)* How are ya.
EDDIE:	*(Indicating Miss Temple)* And this is Rose Marie.
GILBERT:	*(Correcting)* No no, Eddie – Miss Temple.
EDDIE:	*(Acknowledging the protocol)* Oh, quite understand, Mr Donnelly. *(To Una and Joan)* This lady is Miss Temple to you, girls. *(As they turn towards Miss Temple)* That's all right, girls, she can't ... *(Loudly, indicating Sally)* And that's Miss ... ?
GILBERT:	*(Correcting)* That's our Sally.
EDDIE:	*(Acknowledging the protocol)* Oh yeah, quite understand, Mr Donnelly. *(To Una and Joan)* That's Sally, girls, who is temporary and not asked to join in our action. *(To Sally)* Una and Joan from the floor.
SALLY:	Fabulous – how *are* you?
EDDIE:	*(Proudly)* Una here won that prize holiday to ... *(To Una)* where was it?
UNA:	*(Recites)* Bahrain, it's beside Saudia Arabia we went there by Concorde. *(Pause)* I went with me Ma.
JOAN:	She said never again – got sick all the time.
UNA:	*(To Joan)* I did not! *(To all)* No, I liked it all right – but the food was all oily and the Arabs and it used to get real hot and me Ma fell off a camel.
EDDIE:	*(Proudly)* Up on camels they were.
UNA:	Only the once – it was included in the prize – but it was so bumpy that me Ma fainted.
SALLY:	Oh really.
UNA:	And then out in the desert I fainted and all the Arabs had to catch me.
GILBERT:	Ah, the desert. *(Sings)* Blue Heaven and you and I *(Quotes)* and sand kissing a moonlit sky.
UNA:	*(To Gilbert)* Kissing a what?
EDDIE:	Okay, fair enough. Settle in, girls – we all trust that this disruption will be of a short duration. If, in the interim, you have any questions, I'm very sure Mr Donnelly will assist. Mr Donnelly?
GILBERT:	But of course, of course. And we have two handsome bachelors working here too – perhaps you

	know Dave and Liam.
JOAN:	*(Sourly)* Oh, we know them two all right.
SALLY:	*(To Una)* They'll be back in a jiffy.
UNA:	*(To Sally. Friendly)* Dave always has a big rat in his pocket – to frighten us with. I think he's terrible.
JOAN:	*(Of Una)* Don't mind her – she fancies him.
UNA:	*(To Joan)* I do not!
JOAN:	You do so!
UNA:	I do not!
EDDIE:	*(Embarrassed. To Joan and Una)* Manners, girls – manners!
GILBERT:	*(To Eddie and Sally)* Romance could be born of this industrial action.
EDDIE:	Oh, indubiously, indubiously.
GILBERT:	*(To Sally)* Sally, if we're still on strike tomorrow, I'll bring in one of my model railway locos – and some track. Let you see it.
SALLY:	That would be just marvellous, Mr Donnelly.
EDDIE:	Well, I'll be getting back to talk to our members.
JOAN:	*(Quietly)* Hey, Eddie, what about your woman. *(Indicates Miss Temple)* Is she out or not?
EDDIE:	Come here a minute. *(Quietly)* She's out, for the time being – but don't annoy her. She's a tough bird – spent a lot of time in Canada with the Mounties and the Apaches.
JOAN:	*She* did?
EDDIE:	*(To Joan)* She was involved in the knifing of a half-breed but I'm not sure if *she* did it.
JOAN:	*(Aghast)* You're not *sure* ... ?
EDDIE:	Say nothing. *(To all)* I'll leave you so.
GILBERT:	*(To Eddie)* Aye – we'll keep the home fires burning here.
	(Eddie leaves. We see him off along the passageway)
JOAN:	*(To Una)* Not much gas up here, is there? *(Indicates Sally)* Hear the way your woman talks? Jaysus!
UNA:	*(Pause)* Joan, I wish you wouldn't be tellin' them all about me and Dave.
JOAN:	Why not? Aren't you dying to be up here in the offices ... to be near him.
UNA:	I am not.

JOAN:	I know you – you'd love to be working up here with all of them. *(Posh accent)* To be covering your typewriter and going for your elevenses and reading the newspaper. *(Bitterly)* Stuck-up – every one of them is.
UNA:	*(Nervously)* They'll hear you.
JOAN:	Who cares? What are they anyway? *(Indicates Gilbert)* I'd say that oul fella with the hat is bent.
UNA:	*(Annoyed)* Joan, if you don't ...
JOAN:	*(Indicates Miss Temple)* And her? Do you know that she knifed an Indian up in Canada? *(Dave and Liam appear along the corridor. They pause and watch Una and Joan)*
UNA:	*(To Joan)* Will you stop messin'.
JOAN:	You ask Eddie then – that's how she got blinded. *(Dave takes the plastic rat out of his pocket)*
UNA:	Well, I don't believe you and I wish you'd ... *(Dave, holding the rat, rushes into the office. He points it at Una as he chases her)*
UNA:	*(Screams)* Jaysas! *(Runs across the office)*
JOAN:	*(Screams)* Merciful God *(Runs behind a desk)*
DAVE:	*(Chasing Una)* Suas do guna, Una! The big rat will be suas do guna, Una!
UNA:	*(Runs)* Get away, Dave! Mess off, will you ... Jaysas. *(Eventually Una, cornered, bursts into Reynolds' office. Dave stops – puts the rat into his pocket. Silence. Then Una walks out ... followed by Dee)*
DEE:	*(Angrily to Una)* Come here. *(Una advances one pace)* What is your name?
UNA:	Byrne.
DEE:	Byrne. And what do you mean by roaring into this office – by being in this office area at all? *(Silence. To Joan)* And who are you? *(Silence)*
DAVE:	*(To Dee)* The strike, Mrs Kavanagh, is represented on the factory floor *and* in the offices ...
DEE:	*(Angrily)* Sally is not on strike, *I* am not on strike, this office is still open, this area is certainly working a normal day – so why are these members of the factory staff trespassing up here?
DAVE:	*(Sternly)* Mrs Kavanagh, a stand has been made by

	our union ...
DEE:	And it will cost you dearly. (*During next speech, Dave may poise rat over Dee's head, unseen. To Una and Joan*) While both of you must remain in this office, try to remember that you are neither at home nor down on the factory floor. (*Dee goes back to Reynolds' office. Silence*)
JOAN:	(*To Dave*) It was your fault that Una ran in there.
DAVE:	Me? It was my rat that was chasing her. (*Tries to cuddle Una*) He might start chasing her again. Suas do guna, Una.
UNA:	(*To Dave*) Will you mess off.
DAVE:	(*Laughs*) You weren't saying that on Halloween night.
UNA:	(*Giggles*) Shut-up, will you.
	(*Christy enters along the corridor*)
DAVE:	(*To Una*) Will I ask Liam to take out his teeth for you?
LIAM:	Dave!
GILBERT:	Ah-ha, Christy – everything all right?
CHRISTY:	Well, so far so good. Just a few begrudgers making issues out of nothing.
DAVE:	You always get that, Christy.
CHRISTY:	(*Annoyed*) Fellows with long memories – think I'm fighting a private battle with Reynolds (*Bitter laugh*) over *that* job! (*Pause*) Anyway, the point now is that we have a 90% backing on the clerical staff – not bad for un-official action.
DAVE:	I think that's great, Christy. (*Pause*) Oh, you know Una and Joan, don't you?
CHRISTY:	Oh yeah, yeah, hello.
JOAN:	(*To Christy*) You played the bugle at the Christmas party, didn't you?
CHRISTY:	(*Testily*) That was a cornet. (*Awkwardly*) Aren't you Tim Flynn's ... eh ... girlfriend?
DAVE:	(*Suddenly amused*) Are you still going out with Tim Flynn? (*To Liam*) Tim Flynn, remember: put all our bets on the wrong horse in last year's National ...
JOAN:	You're a liar – he did not!
DAVE:	He *did*. Sure last month when we all went to that funeral up in Glasnevin, didn't *he* follow the wrong coffin ... over to *Mount Jerome*. And then when we

114

	asked him about it ...
JOAN:	*(Furiously)* Yes, go on – make them up. You're all so bloody smart up here in the offices. Well, let me tell you that Tim Flynn is a better man than any of you will ever be! So shag off! *(Goes angrily out onto the passageway. Closes the door. Gazes down at the factory below)*
DAVE:	I know what she wants – and Tim Flynn must be getting *that* wrong too.
LIAM:	*(To Christy. Anxiously)* He *is* coming out, isn't he? Tim Flynn? The Beltman?
CHRISTY:	*(Furious at Dave, but controlled)* Yes, he is.
LIAM:	*(Anxiously)* My God, he'll have to. If he doesn't, we're really sunk because the drivers ...
CHRISTY:	*(Shouts angrily)* He's coming out – weren't you told that? What more do you want? If you'd all just shut-up and do what you're told, we'd get this thing settled. *(Silence)*
LIAM:	*(Quietly)* We stay in here, Christy, do we?
CHRISTY:	*(Controlled again)* Yes, we ... sit-in. Take turns to go out for meals. Someone will ... *I'll* probably stay overnight. Maybe ... maybe we best arrange the dinnershift right away. You know – stagger it by half-an-hour to keep it covered.
DAVE:	Well – we could slip off now ...
GILBERT:	Aye – and I'll go in half-an-hour then – give me time to help Miriam prepare the railway lay-out for Albert tonight.
LIAM:	*(Hesitantly to Dave)* Maybe if I ... ?
CHRISTY:	*(Testily)* Just sort it out between you. *(To Una)* You better tell your ... tell Joan about the meal-breaks.
DAVE:	*(Prepares to leave. To Una)* If you want to go now, we can drive you.
UNA:	*(To Dave as she goes out to Joan)* Oh – I'll ask Joan.
LIAM:	Dave, maybe if I took the half-hour *after* Gilbert, it would be ...
DAVE:	*(To Liam)* And how are you getting back to the flat? Taking two buses?
LIAM:	*(Looks at Sally)* Well, I was thinking that Sally and I might just get something to eat down at ...
DAVE:	*(Angry)* Oh I see. *(To Sally)* You're sure you won't be

too *afraid* to do that.

UNA:	*(Hesitantly from the passageway)* Eh Dave?
DAVE:	*(To Una)* Right – come on.
UNA:	Dave, Joan says she won't ... go with you – and I ...
DAVE:	What am I – a leper or something?
JOAN:	*(To Una)* You can go with him.
DAVE:	You both live in the same block, don't you? Come on.
UNA:	*(To Joan)* Come on.
JOAN:	*(Following)* He looks like a bleedin' leper to me.
DAVE:	*(Angrily to Joan)* Get Tim Flynn to bring you home then.
JOAN:	*(Angrily to Dave)* I would if ...
DAVE:	*(Viciously)* Yes – you'd look sweet up on his crossbar.
JOAN:	Ah shag off. *(Dave, Una and Joan go)*
CHRISTY:	*(Gently)* Eh, Miss Temple – going around, I found that there is a feeling among the members that ... eh ... in your condition, there is ... is no obligation on you to withdraw labour till the delegates come and ...
MISS TEMPLE:	Oh, but I'd prefer to support this action, Mr Metcalf. I've always felt that you – and not Mr Reynolds should have got that job.
CHRISTY:	*(Testily)* Well, thank you – but that's not the issue here.
MISS TEMPLE:	Ah, but it is. If you *had* got that job, we would not be in this situation now. Someone's coming.
	(We see Mike Reynolds and Ronnie Partridge coming along the passageway. Mr Partridge is sixty, elegant)
CHRISTY:	Someone's ...? *(Sees Reynolds and Partridge)* It's Reynolds and ... oh, Jesus.
MISS TEMPLE:	And who?
CHRISTY:	Mr Partridge himself!
	(Reynolds and Partridge enter)
PARTRIDGE:	*(Immediately and angrily to Gilbert)* Now Gilbert – what is this? Don't tell me *you're* on strike!
GILBERT:	Ah Ronnie – do you know that Albert and Gladys have arrived ...
PARTRIDGE:	To hell with Albert and Gladys – are *you* on strike?
GILBERT:	Aye – I am, I am.
PARTRIDGE:	*(Furious)* But how the blazes can *you* be on strike? The blasted strike is against you!

GILBERT:	Me? Ah, no no, Ronnie ...
PARTRIDGE:	No no nothing! There is a picket on the plant and there is a blasted sit-in because you correctly dismissed a man for refusing to perform his duties. Is that not so? Of course it is! Now explain to me how you can be on strike against yourself?
GILBERT:	Aye Ronnie – but my union ...
PARTRIDGE:	To hell with your union ...
CHRISTY:	*(Offended)* Now, Mr Partridge ...
PARTRIDGE:	*(To Christy)* I'll come to you in a moment. *(To Gilbert)* You're on strike against yourself, Gilbert – you're being made to look like a fool. If ... if they carry banners saying 'Death to Gilbert Donnelly' are you going to carry one too? If they decide to burn your effigy, are you going to light the match? Don't be a blasted idiot, Gilbert – I'm amazed at you. *(To all)* I'm amazed at any one of my staff behaving like this – a staff that is handpicked for its good character, responsible attitude, common sense ...
CHRISTY:	Now, Mr Partridge ...
PARTRIDGE:	*(Disgusted. To Christy)* You! Oh yes, you. I remember *you* at the interview – and it doesn't surprise me that *you're* behind this ... this *childishness*.
CHRISTY:	It's not childishness ...
PARTRIDGE:	Look, get these people back to work ...
CHRISTY:	Let me finish, Mr Partridge – as and from one o'clock today ...
PARTRIDGE:	I will *not* let you finish. Cut out this refusing to work and get these people back to their jobs. You are already demoralising a good staff. You ... you have factory girls in offices; unfortunate creatures *(Indicates Miss Temple)* on strike for something they can't possibly know anything about; a man picketing himself ... Get some sense – get back to work. *(To Reynolds)* Where are we, Mike?
REYNOLDS:	*(Indicates his office)* This way, Mr Partridge.
CHRISTY:	Now, Mr Partridge – as and from one o'clock today ...
PARTRIDGE:	*(Turns. To Christy)* You can't win. The drivers are working, the conveyor belts are working, there are sufficient supplies on the belt to load the ship ... you

	can't win.
REYNOLDS:	Mr Partridge (*Whispers briefly. Indicates Liam*)
GILBERT:	Albert was saying that perhaps some evening we'd ...
PARTRIDGE:	(*To Liam*) The staff in this factory is chosen meticulously. If you want to remain part of it – do what you're told and do it quickly.
	(*Partridge and Reynolds enter Reynolds' office. Door is closed*)
LIAM:	(*Panic*) What does he mean? My God, if they win, we're finished – you and I and ...
CHRISTY:	Shut-up Liam. We're all right. This is the way they operate. They're in there now waiting for us to crack ... to come crawling to them.
LIAM:	But is the Beltman working or not?
CHRISTY:	I told you – the belt will be turned off by Tim Flynn at one o'clock and won't be turned on again. And without the belt, nothing moves.
GILBERT:	(*Pause*) Never saw Ronnie so upset since the day in London when that tattooist used an un-hygienic needle and ... oh dear, his poor chest ... (*Indicates his chest.*
	(*Eddie appears on the passageway. Enters*)
EDDIE:	Afternoon gents – everything in order?
LIAM:	(*Anxiously*) Mr Partridge has been saying ...
CHRISTY:	(*Calmly*) Oh – Partridge and Reynolds arrived with their usual threats ...
EDDIE:	No sweat there, gents – that's par for the course at this stage. O-kay – we have the picket on the gate, complete solidarity on the floor. (*To Christy*) You'll stay here tonight?
LIAM:	(*Anxiously*) And the Beltman – he's coming out is he?
CHRISTY:	(*To Eddie*) Yes, I'll bring back a sleeping bag, put it down somewhere here ... I ... I'll get the neighbours to keep an eye on the mother – they usually do that if I'm late at the boys' club or ...
EDDIE:	Game ball – I'll be doing the ...
LIAM:	(*Very anxious*) Eddie, the Beltman *is* turning off the conveyors at dinner hour, isn't he?
EDDIE:	(*Continuing to Christy*) I'll be doing the night turn below myself. (*To Liam*) The what?

LIAM:	It is ... being turned off at dinner-hour?
EDDIE:	*(Pause)* The belt? Well, in point of fact – no, it's not.
GILBERT:	It's not?
MISS TEMPLE:	It's not?
LIAM:	It's *not?*
CHRISTY:	*(Suddenly anxious)* It's not? But it must ... I told the offices that ... you ... *you* assured *me* that ...
EDDIE:	*(Loudly)* The reason ... *(Calmly)* The reason, gents, is that the Beltman, Tim Flynn, sent word that he can't get here at dinner-hour. He says he broke the frames of his glasses. He's delayed so the belt will not be turned off at dinner-hour.
LIAM:	Why? *(Shouts)* He *always* turns it off at dinner hour! Why not today?
EDDIE:	*(Angrily)* He's delayed, pal – and nobody else has the key and nobody else can turn it off – union rules. It'll go off this evening – and it won't go on tomorrow. That's guaranteed. Okay?
CHRISTY:	Eddie, the men expect ... there's a lot at stake here – my reputation, your reputation ...
	(Partridge, Dee and Reynolds come from the office. They cross smugly and silently to the exit door. We see Partridge and Dee go)
REYNOLDS:	*(As he leaves. Smugly to Christy)* Once a loser, always a loser.
CHRISTY:	Who's a loser?
REYNOLDS:	*(Pauses. Sarcastic)* Oh, hasn't it sunk in yet? You're finished. *(Leaves smartly)*
CHRISTY:	*(Furious but unconvincing)* Don't be so sure ...
LIAM:	*(Bitterly)* Jesus, I knew it. We're sunk. *(Shouts at Christy)* I shouldn't have bloody listened to you! *(Miss Temple turns and sits at the switch)*
CHRISTY:	*(Confused)* Me? For God's sake, Liam, what did I ...? tomorrow will be all right – you heard Eddie. The belt will be turned off. *(To Eddie)* Won't it?
MISS TEMPLE:	*(Into phone)* Donnycarney Metal Works.
CHRISTY:	*(To Miss Temple)* Hey, what the hell are you ... ?
MISS TEMPLE:	*(Quietly)* You said I could if I wished.
CHRISTY:	*(Panic)* Miss Temple, get away from that – get away from ...

EDDIE: *(Takes Christy's arm)* Leave her Christy, leave her. *(To all)* Okay fair enough, we've had a set-back – but all it means is that delivery continues for an extra half-day that is all. There's no sweat.

LIAM: We're sunk! We're sunk!

(Gilbert looks through the window at the factory)

MISS TEMPLE: *(Into the PA)* Would the fork-lift operators please clear the delivery area. Thank you. *(Switches off the PA)*

CHRISTY: *(Furiously to Eddie)* Eddie – I don't want her working on now that the Beltman is not going to ... *(To Miss Temple)* Miss Temple ... !

EDDIE: *(Shouts)* Christy! *(Quietly)* Trust me, Christy – I know what I'm talking about. Leave her be. We have a fight on our hands against Partridge now – so this is not the time to take on an unfortunate woman who was blinded knifing Indians up in Canada.

CHRISTY: *(Aghast)* What ... Indians?!

EDDIE: *(Angrily)* I know what I'm talking about, Christy – we'll deal with her later. *Later.* All right? Okay?

MISS TEMPLE: Fair enough.

(Christy panics again. Liam is totally dejected. Eddie looks suspiciously at Miss Temple)

FADE OUT
END OF ACT ONE

ACT TWO

Scene One

Same set. It is the following day – early morning. Very quiet. Nothing moves. Hold for fifteen seconds. We see Eddie coming along the passage-way. He opens the door and switches on the office lights. He is dressed in a fashionable three-piece suit. He is neat, well-groomed. He carries a tray of two bowls, breakfast cereal and milk. He also carries a dart board which he hangs up.

EDDIE: Mornin' *(Louder)* Mornin' *(Shouts)* Christy!
(There is a sudden commotion at the switchboard wall. We now see Christy struggle in his sleeping bag. There is an old alarm clock beside his head. He wears old-fashioned striped pyjamas)

CHRISTY: My God – what time is it? *(Picks up clock)*

EDDIE: *(Checks his watch)* Eight forty-four.

CHRISTY: *(Puts clock down)* The mother always has this thing a half-an-hour slow. *(On his feet, still in the sleeping bag)* You slept down on the factory floor?

EDDIE: Certainly I did. *(Puts on his jacket)*

CHRISTY: *(Suddenly)* The belts! The machines! *(Jumps awkward-ly to the window)* The conveyor belt is stopped.

EDDIE: *(Confidently)* Should've been on at eight.

CHRISTY: Tim Flynn – the Beltman – he's not turning them on then?

EDDIE: He's not ... *(Proudly)* ....because representations were made by a third party on our behalf and, *ipso facto,* Tim Flynn is today joining our union. So complete solidarity.

CHRISTY: He's joining your union?

EDDIE: Complete solidarity. And now I suggest you put on some clothes before the ladies arrive.
(While Eddie sits at Gilbert's desk to arrange breakfast, he will be amused to see Christy try to modestly change from his pyjamas by standing/sitting/rolling in the sleeping-bag. This performance begins with him extracting a hot-

121

water bottle and continues as)

CHRISTY: Eddie, this is great. This puts a different complexion on everything.

EDDIE: Put that to music, Christy, and you could get your boys to play it on their ukuleles.

CHRISTY: *(Pause)* Their cornets, Eddie.

EDDIE: Oh yeah – whatever they are. Okay fair enough, we had our set-backs yesterday and, as I said then, that's par for the course on the implementation of any industrial action.

CHRISTY: *(As he struggles to dress)* Yes, you did say that. *(Pause)* But, to be honest, Eddie, I was getting a bit worried – you ... you don't want to disappoint the men when ... when they trust you.

EDDIE: Oh indubiously, Christy – but, take my word, they'll soon be very proud of you.

CHRISTY: Yes. *(Very friendly)* And you, Eddie.

EDDIE: Thank you, Christy. Well, we still have to put the screws on Partridge. That'll make our members really proud.

CHRISTY: Ho ho, yes. And those begrudgers will come out now for sure – those smart-alecks who said that the company would laugh at us. They'll change now.

EDDIE: Certainly. Everyone will want to be on your side now – everyone loves a winner.

CHRISTY: *(Is now dressed as he was yesterday. Steps from the bag)* And we've a great chance of official sanction too – have the branch secretary in today probably.

EDDIE: Oh, no sweat there now. Okay fair enough – they're cautious at the beginning – but they'll back the workers 100% when the situation becomes ...

CHRISTY: *(Throws his pyjamas under Liam's desk)* ... apparent.

EDDIE: ... serious. When it becomes serious. And Partridge will have to crawl now. We've been pushed as far as we'll go.

CHRISTY: *(Joins Eddie eating)* I just want to see the face of Reynolds ... and that bitch Dee Kavanagh ...

EDDIE: Yeah. *(Pause)* Mother all right?

CHRISTY: Ah, bit anxious when she heard I'd be out for the night – started getting the pains – but, the neighbours

	... *(Feels his chin)* Oh, should have brought a razor.
EDDIE:	Razor? Now, you slip down to my locker, Christy – *(Throws the key)* and use my electric – towels and soap there too, if you want ... all packed by the little woman.
CHRISTY:	*(Pause. Thoughtfully)* You have her ... eh ... well trained. She wasn't anxious ... at you being ...?
EDDIE:	Nothing for her to be anxious about – because she knew nothing. Same as when we all go off on the darts or pitch-and-putt trips – just tell her I'll be away for a few days and she packs the bag. Then it's 'good luck, love' and a few bob for the kids. Anything else only invites trouble.
CHRISTY:	Yes. *(Decided)* Well, I'll take you up on the locker ... Eddie.
EDDIE:	Number 36 – it's on the key – red ones, on the left.
CHRISTY:	*(Collects the dishes, picks up the tray)* I'll run these under the tap while I'm down there.
EDDIE:	Game ball, Christy.
CHRISTY:	*(At the door. Amused. Indicates the key)* Eddie – red ones: on the left.
EDDIE:	*(Raises a fist. Laughs)* On the left, Christy. No sweat there.
	(Christy goes out and off along the passageway. Eddie watches him go. Then he relaxes in the empty office: playing with machines, sitting into the chairs. Then he merrily picks up Gilbert's phone)
EDDIE:	*(In great humour, into phone)* Hello. Malone speakin'. Youse are all fired! *(Slams phone down. Highly amused)* Bleedin' unions!
	(As Eddie confidently walks around, tapping keyboards, etc., we see Gilbert arrive. Eddie immediately hides along the corridor. Gilbert is casually dressed. Probably in tweeds. He still wears his hat. He carries a large cardboard carton)
GILBERT:	*(Enters. Looks around. Quotes)* Oh, what a beautiful morning, oh what a beautiful day *(sings with great feeling)* Oh, what a beautiful morning, oh what a beautiful day, I got a beautiful feeling ... *(Pause. Repeats to check pitch)* feeling. *(Satisfied)* Everything's going my

	way. Oh the cattle are standin' like statues, oh the cattle are ...
EDDIE:	*(Coming from corridor)* Mornin', Mr Donnelly.
GILBERT:	*(Surprised)* Ah Eddie – Nelson Eddy – didn't notice you there. Aye.
EDDIE:	You're in good voice this morning, Mr Donnelly ... *(Proudly indicating the belts)* ... and I think I know why.
GILBERT:	Aye – because the air is drier today; keeps the voice on key. *(Complimentary)* You've a very good musical ear, Eddie.
EDDIE:	*(Disgusted)* Yeah. *(Tries again)* Talking of ears, did you notice anything ... *(Indicates the factory)*
GILBERT:	*(Pre-occupied. Opening the carton)* Brought this in for Sally. *(Holds up a model locomotive. Proudly)* The Duchess of Sutherland. And some track.
EDDIE:	*(Amazed)* A toy train? Your son's, is it?
GILBERT:	*(Begins to set up the track)* My ...? No no, no sons. Mine. Once you've been bitten by the bug, Eddie, you'll never want anything else – running the perfect service, taking decisions, in complete control. Chum of mine, Albert White, was over last night – oh, we ran a wonderful service.
EDDIE:	*(Amazed)* He has a train as well?
GILBERT:	Oh aye – Albert's a great collector: locos, bridges, marshalling yards, viaducts – aye, and he brought over his old Southern Region uniform too, cap and tunic. Looked splendid – in complete control. *(Pause)* You don't have a train yourself, do you, Eddie?
EDDIE:	*(Offended)* A train? No, I don't. The eldest lad at home has one though.
GILBERT:	Oh?
EDDIE:	*(Hard)* He's seven! *(Pause)* Did you notice anything about the factory.
GILBERT:	Oh aye, aye. *(Pause)* What's that Eddie?
EDDIE:	*(Annoyed)* We stopped the conveyor belt in the factory.
GILBERT:	*(Looks out)* My word – so you have. How did that happen?
EDDIE:	*(Disgusted)* Mr Donnelly, someone was saying that for you this job, this whole place, is a bit of a hobby, that you're retiring to Jersey soon – where your wife

	comes from. *(Pause)*
GILBERT:	*(Returning to set-up the tracks)* You're quite right Eddie – Miriam is from St Helier in Jersey – and Gladys is from St Peter Port. That's Guernsey. Aye. *(Dave and Liam come running along the passageway. Both are casually dressed in sweaters and jeans. Liam carries a radio)*
LIAM:	*(Enters. Announces)* Behold – a silence like the second day of creation!
DAVE:	*(Laughing)* Not a sound is heard – not a bird singing.
LIAM:	Or a conveyor belt conveying! *(Cheers. To Eddie)* Put it there, Eddie. *(Shakes hands)* I was sick to my stomach this morning in case ...
DAVE:	*(To Eddie)* Walking around at half-five ... no breakfast ... *(Indicates Liam)*
LIAM:	God, I couldn't touch breakfast ... I felt physically sick in case I'd hear that belt clanking away ...
DAVE:	*(Laughs)* I told him – have faith in your union ...
EDDIE:	Oh, indubiously.
LIAM:	No – it was just that all yesterday afternoon, sitting up here hearing that belt going ... and those bastards loading the consignments ...
EDDIE:	Well now – having the drivers working gives us more bargaining clout.
DAVE:	*(To Eddie)* How did you stop the belt? *(Miss Temple appears along the passageway)*
EDDIE:	*(Proudly)* Gentlemen, representations were made and from today Tim Flynn will be part of our union. Complete solidarity.
DAVE:	*(To Eddie. Delighted)* You got him to join our ... ? Jas, that's terrific. *(Liam turns on the radio. Miss Temple enters)*
MISS TEMPLE:	Good morning, Gilbert. *(Hangs her coat)*
GILBERT:	Ah, Miss Temple.
MISS TEMPLE:	Very seasonal this morning. *(Hears the music)* Oh, such nice music. *(Sets off down stage towards the switch – and the track)*
GILBERT:	*(Runs to her)* No, no, Miss Temple. *(Takes her arm)* This way this morning, if you please. *(Leads her. Now excitedly)* I've brought in the Duchess of Sutherland.

125

MISS TEMPLE:	*(Delighted)* Oh – down there, is she?
GILBERT:	Yes, she is. And some track too.
MISS TEMPLE:	Lovely, Gilbert.
	(Christy enters. There follows great hysteria as Dave and Liam grab Christy, eventually carry him and all collapse on the floor. The radio plays loudly)
LIAM:	*(Rushing to Christy. Hugs him)* Belt, I command you to stop, he said – and it stopped!
DAVE:	*(Hugging Christy)* Lift him shoulder-high. Speech! Speech!
CHRISTY:	*(Delighted)* Hold on, lads – hold on. Eddie here should take some credit.
EDDIE:	No, no, it's your moment, Christy. It's your moment. *(Dee Kavanagh enters. She switches off the radio. All stop. She watches Dave and Liam, on the floor with Christy)*
DEE:	*(Sweetly)* Have I interrupted something? *(Christy quickly moves away from Dave and Liam)* Oh, I see – just one of the strike leaders having a gay old time.
GILBERT:	Good morning, Dee.
DEE:	Good morning, Mr Donnelly ... and train. *(Pointed)* I wondered if you were having trouble separating the men from the boys this morning.
CHRISTY:	*(Forced laugh)* Doesn't work anymore, Mrs Kavanagh. That kind of allegation is ignored now.
DEE:	Really? By whom?
CHRISTY:	The factory and the belts are stopped. We make the allegations now.
DEE:	*(Moves away)* Oh carry-on, Mr Metcalf – I won't say I saw anything. Your little secret is safe. *(Goes into Reynolds' office)*
CHRISTY:	*(Furiously)* And what about you and Reynolds! *(Dee closes the door)* Bitch! *(Awkwardly to all)* It ... it's a twisted mind that jumps to those kind of conclusions ...
EDDIE:	Take it easy, pal – she's only going on like that because the belt is stopped – trying to provoke us.
CHRISTY:	*(Quietly)* If a fellow isn't chasing bits of skirt all day ... if he stays home to look after his mother ...
EDDIE:	Ignore her, pal. Look – we all go through that at one time or another. Take me: I lived at home with the Ma (God be good to her) until I was over eighteen,

126

	'till I met the mot, in fact – and then we got married, settled down, had a few kids and so on. Okay fair enough, I moved out then – but nobody said anything while I was there, did they? I mean, while I lived with the Ma, there was no reflection on me – and if there was, I ignored it. So – why worry?
MISS TEMPLE:	*(Quietly)* That's nonsense.
EDDIE:	*(Aggressively)* What's that, lady?
MISS TEMPLE:	You're talking about a totally different situation.
EDDIE:	It's the same situation – if you'd listen.
MISS TEMPLE:	It's totally different.
EDDIE:	*(Shouts)* It is not ... totally different.
DAVE:	*(Awkward pause)* Well, it's like Liam here. *(To Liam)* You lived with your Ma before you moved into the flat.
LIAM:	*(Angrily to Dave)* For God's sake, that was because I couldn't be travelling forty miles every day.
DAVE:	I know, isn't that what I said.
LIAM:	Well then?
CHRISTY:	*(Uneasily. Immediately)* Right. All right. Anyway, thanks for the shave, Eddie *(Gives him his keys)*
EDDIE:	Oh – game ball, Christy. *(Pause. Now relaxed. To all)* Look – I think we should keep this in mind, gents – they want us to be rowing between ourselves and my advice to all of us is: ignore them and we all stay friends. Overlook our differences. And that applies to us all, in toto. *(To Miss Temple)* So, put it there, lady. *(Shakes hands with her. To all)* There. Okay?
MISS TEMPLE:	Fair enough.
EDDIE:	Okay, Christy?
CHRISTY:	Suppose you're right. *(Takes the clock and sleeping bag as he goes off along the corridor)* Back in a minute. *(As he passes the window of Reynolds' office. Quietly)* Bitch.
GILBERT:	*(To Miss Temple)* Miss Temple, had Albert and Gladys over last night.
MISS TEMPLE:	Oh – did he bring his railway?
GILBERT:	Aye – just his French loco and some coaches. And we sang the Mounties song again. *(Sings)* 'Out on the trail, like a pack of hungry wolves on the trail'.
MISS TEMPLE:	I'd like to have heard that, Gilbert, 'The Son of the

	Mounties'.
GILBERT:	Aye – well, we must have you over some time – before Albert and Gladys go back.
EDDIE:	*(Very friendly to Miss Temple)* Eh, Miss Temple, I believe you do a very admirable rendition yourself of 'The Apache Love Song'
MISS TEMPLE:	I beg your pardon?
EDDIE:	*(Nods to Gilbert)* I hear it's your party-piece – 'The Apache Love Song'.
GILBERT:	*(Lost)* Aye – is it? Well now, I never heard that one – and neither did I hear you singing it, Miss Temple.
MISS TEMPLE:	I rarely sing. And I never heard of that song either.
EDDIE:	*(Nodding to Gilbert)* Remember? The Mounties and all ... the Saloon ... 'The Apache Love Song'?
GILBERT:	Ah, the Mounties! The only song I know of that nature is 'The Indian Love Call'.
EDDIE:	That's it. 'The Indian Love Call'.
MISS TEMPLE:	'The Indian Love Call'?
GILBERT:	Aye, from *Rose Marie*.
EDDIE:	Yeah, that's what I said *(Indicates Miss Temple)* from *Rose Marie*.
MISS TEMPLE:	*(Quietly to Gilbert)* I think he's confusing me with Jeanette MacDonald.
	(Una and Joan appear along the passageway. They are now very fashionably dressed)
EDDIE:	*(To Miss Temple)* Jeanette MacDonald? *(To Gilbert)* Is she clerical or factory?
DAVE:	*(Sees Una and Joan)* Jesus – will you look at what's coming in now.
EDDIE:	*(Proudly)* Good morning, girls.
JOAN:	*(Entering)* Morning.
UNA:	*(Shyly)* Hello.
GILBERT:	Well, well, well – I must say that you young ladies are looking very pretty this morning.
JOAN:	*(Sourly)* Yeah? We have good gear too, you know.
LIAM:	Yes, indeed.
DAVE:	*(Looking closely at Una)* Very nice, Una – and, may I add, that's a very convenient zip you have there. *(Reaches towards her)*
UNA:	*(Giggles)* Mess off, will you, Dave.

GILBERT: *(Quotes)* Two little maids from school. *(To Eddie)* Eh, Eddie?

EDDIE: Oh, indubiously.

DAVE: *(Moving after Una)* Have you got those padded up ...?

UNA: Will you ... Dave! Everyone's looking ...

DAVE: *(Still after her)* If I had my rat with me ... *(Grabs Una)*

JOAN: *(Suddenly)* Cut it out – you'd leave her alone quick enough if you knew ...

UNA: *(Sharply)* Joan!

DAVE: *(Laughing)* What? What is it?

UNA: *(To Joan)* Shut-up, will you.

DAVE: *(Laughing)* What is it?

UNA: Nothing.

EDDIE: *(Loudly to all)* Gentlemen, may I interrupt. *(Solemnly)* A word of gratitude, I think, now to Joan here who, on our behalf, relayed our proposal to Tim Flynn that he join our union and, officially support our stoppage. Thank you, Joan. *(Begins an applause)* I think so? *(All applaud)*

LIAM: Yes indeed.

UNA: *(Slaps Joan on the back)* Hurrah!

JOAN: *(Embarrassed)* Mess of – I only had to tell him.

EDDIE: *(With flair)* That won't be forgotten, Joan *(Steps back to make the point)* ... and as soon as Tim has signed the forms, et cetera this morning, we may be able to have him up here with ... *(Steps towards Gilbert's track)*

GILBERT: *(Suddenly taking a loco from Eddie's path)* Careful where you walk ...

EDDIE: *(Angrily)* Ah Jaysas, what the ...? *(Moves away)* Bleedin' toy trains!

UNA: Who owns it anyway?

DAVE: That's Mr Donnelly's toy train.

UNA: *(Not believing)* Mess off, will you.

DAVE: *(Laughs)* It is!

EDDIE: Any objections, gents, if I take a look around the other offices while we're ...?

MISS TEMPLE: *(Stands. Indicates)* Not at all. They're directly down that corridor, through the second door on the left – that's the one with the glass panels – and then first right. *(Pause. Sits)* You can't miss them. *(Eddie is*

129

	amazed/suspicious)
JOAN:	Eddie, will we go with you?
EDDIE:	Eh no *(Recovers)* No, you two stay here on duty – you're factory floor representatives.
JOAN:	*(Annoyed)* I know we're factory floor representatives, but can't we go with you to ...?
EDDIE:	No! Your duties, girls, are on this office floor, so you remain here. *(Loudly)* All right?
UNA:	*(Quietly)* All right.
JOAN:	*(Annoyed)* All right. *(As Eddie goes)* Jaysas.
UNA:	*(Watches Eddie go. Now excited again)* Ah, come on, now – who owns it? No messin'.
DAVE:	It's Mr Donnelly's train all right.
GILBERT:	*(Hearing this. Proudly)* Aye. That's my Duchess of Sutherland.
JOAN:	*(To Una)* What did he say?
DAVE:	*(Playing it up)* That's Mr Donnelly's Duchess. That engine.
GILBERT:	Aye – loco. It was Glasgow to Euston from 1936 to 1960. Irreplaceable now.
UNA:	*(To Joan)* He says it's his Duchess.
JOAN:	*(Laughing quietly)* And he plays with it up here? *(Sudden hysterics)* While we're making tools down there, he's playing with his Duchess up here!
DAVE:	*(Playing it up)* And you built the track all around the house, didn't you Gilbert?
GILBERT:	Aye – the lay-out: cross-overs, a shunting siding off a dog-bone loop ...
JOAN:	*(To Una)* A dog-bone loop!
UNA:	*(Bursting)* Jesus! Shut-up!
GILBERT:	... and I log all the derailments during every operation – check all accidents – snap decisions – in total control ...
	(We see Sally approaching)
JOAN:	*(Suppressing laughter. Indicates the train)* And does this really go?
GILBERT:	Oh aye – as soon as I find the power-point to plug it in, my dear. *(Takes the flex to beside the switchboard. On his knees. Searches behind the switch for a connection)* It'll reach the one here by the switchboard.

SALLY:	*(Entering)* Good morning. I'm afraid my watch stopped.
LIAM:	So has the belt. Did you notice?
SALLY:	Oh yes, I did.
UNA:	*(Happily to Sally)* And we're staying up here until it's all settled. *(Proudly)* In the offices.
SALLY:	Lovely. *(To Gilbert)* And the train! Mr Donnelly, you brought in your train!
GILBERT:	Aye – just looking for a power-point here to get her rolling. *(Searches)* Seems to be broken.
SALLY:	*(Looking at the track)* Isn't it just fabulous?
	(Dee comes from Reynolds' office)
DEE:	Oh hello, Sally – glad you're in.
SALLY:	Oh good morning, Mrs Kavanagh – I'm afraid I mistook the time and ...
DEE:	That's all right, Sally. *(Produces a file)* Look, we'll have to make adjustments now in all our prospective marketing analysis. I'll leave it with you ...
SALLY:	*(Takes file)* Of course – I'll do it right away.
DEE:	You can work at my desk, if you like – I'll use Mike's office. *(Pause)* Will you just look at them!
GILBERT:	*(Searching for a power-point)* Ah, loose wire here.
DEE:	*(Quietly to Sally)* Mr Partridge is coming in later – and Mike – we think there is something that can be done to ... clip their wings.
	(Dee returns to Reynolds' office)
UNA:	*(Having been whispering to Joan)* I'll ask Dave. *(Calls)* Dave!
DAVE:	*(Hears this)* Yes?
UNA:	*(Indicates Gilbert. Quietly)* Joan wants to know why he wears that hat.
JOAN:	I don't.
GILBERT:	*(To Miss Temple)* Are you getting any sound from the board, Miss Temple?
MISS TEMPLE:	*(Touches the switches)* No Gilbert – we've had no calls at all this morning.
UNA:	*(To Dave)* Is he baldy or what?
DAVE:	*(Quietly but with relish)* He's as bald as an egg, girls.
LIAM:	*(Annoyed)* He's not.
DAVE:	*(Quickly)* Not what?

131

LIAM:	He's not bald.
DAVE:	*(Aggressively)* How do you know? *(Pause)* Well?
LIAM:	*(Reluctantly)* Because ... because he has a brush and comb in his desk. I saw it.
DAVE:	*(Recovers. Laughs)* And what does that prove? You have toothpaste and a toothbrush in the flat – but that doesn't say you have front teeth! *(Cuddles Una)* Eh, Una? Dracula – eh?
LIAM:	*(Angrily)* For Christ's sake, Dave ...
GILBERT:	*(Loudly. From behind the board)* Ah – all of the connections are out of the board here.
LIAM:	*(Looks up)* They're what?
GILBERT:	Aye – all the connecting lines are out ...
SALLY:	The phone inside is. *(Indicates Reynolds' office)*
LIAM:	That's a different circuit, I think. *(Goes to the switch)* But these should be all right. *(Kneels down)* This one is *broken* off ... *(Dave goes to the switch. Eddie and Christy arrive back along the corridor. They are examining Eddie's darts)*
EDDIE:	*(To Christy)* They're the Tumson darts, Christy – they're very good.
CHRISTY:	Yes – and that left him with a double sixteen.
LIAM:	Christy, the plugs at the switchboard have been either disconnected or broken ...
EDDIE:	*(To Christy)* So I need a treble eighteen, double top ...
LIAM:	Christy, the plugs have been either disconnected or broken ...
DAVE:	Most of them are in bits.
LIAM:	As if someone ...
CHRISTY:	*(To Eddie)* What? Well ... *(Quietly)* Well, I couldn't ...
EDDIE:	*(Pause. Authoritatively)* Okay, if there is any electrical fault, gents, it is not our function to repair them. Okay fair enough if there is *danger* – fire or shock or short-circuit. Is there danger?
LIAM:	If someone touches them ...
EDDIE:	Then don't touch them. Okay? *(Loudly. Finally)* No one is to touch any malfunction in any department here. That is not our job. Our job here is to be on strike.
CHRISTY:	Here, here.

132

DAVE:	Exactly. *(To Liam)* Leave it as it is. *(Takes up his news-paper)* We'll have question-time.
EDDIE:	Question-time?
GILBERT:	Aye – I just needed power to run the loco ...
CHRISTY:	*(Sarcastic to Gilbert)* I think we can forget your loco and ...
DAVE:	Yeah – come on: question-time now *(Opens his paper)*
EDDIE:	*(Conclusively)* Right. *(To Christy, anxiously)* What sort of question-time are we talking about?
LIAM:	But if we could just connect the lead from the train to ...
CHRISTY:	Look Liam – we're on strike here ...
MISS TEMPLE:	*(Suddenly stands. She has put on rubber gloves)* Well, I'm not on strike – I'll fix it. *(Takes a pincers and screw-driver from her bag)*
GILBERT:	*(Anxiously)* Oh no no, Miss Temple – there's really no need ...
MISS TEMPLE:	*(Climbs to the fuse box)* No Gilbert – you brought in your railway and we shall have it going. Give me the plug. *(Unscrews the lid of the fuse-box)*
CHRISTY:	Miss Temple – you're not supposed to ... *(To Eddie)* She can't be ...
EDDIE:	*(Angrily)* Yes – leave it, lady. You'll fry yourself up at that fuse-box. Get down right away!
MISS TEMPLE:	*(Feels across the fuses)* Now let's see ...
JOAN:	*(Nervously)* Jaysas – look at her.
MISS TEMPLE:	The fuses are all there – all nice and tight.
CHRISTY:	Eddie, we can't be letting her fix the ...
EDDIE:	*(Furiously and authoritatively)* Yes, all right, all right!! Miss Temple? I am instructing you on behalf of the union committee to get away from that electricity. There's a strike on here.
MISS TEMPLE:	*(Getting down beside the switchboard)* Oh, Mr Malone – it's not a railway strike. *(Quietly)* I'll check the leads next.
CHRISTY:	The leads?!
EDDIE:	*(Shouts)* Miss Temple, I'm warning you! You're breaking the strike in this office ... !
JOAN:	*(Shouts)* Jaysas, she's holding the wires ... !
UNA:	*(Panic)* Oh mammy ...
DAVE:	*(Nervously)* Miss Temple – you're going to kill your-

	self ...
CHRISTY:	*(Angrily to all)* Someone should stop her before she ...
EDDIE:	*(To Christy)* Yes! All right! *(Runs to Miss Temple)* Right! I warned you! *(Tries to lift her)* Now, get away from that switchboard! Get away from it!
MISS TEMPLE:	*(Screams)* Don't you touch me! *(Turns, holding out the screwdriver)*
EDDIE:	*(Jumps back. Angrily)* I'm not afraid of you – I'm not afraid of you ... or the Indians. I know all about Black Eagle – the half-breed you knifed up in Canada. I know all about that ...
SALLY:	What?
LIAM:	What?
	(Suddenly Gilbert blows his whistle, the current is connected and the train goes off along the track)
UNA:	*(Pause. Now delighted)* Jaysas look – look at it.
SALLY:	Oh isn't it nice? Watch out! *(Gently moves Liam away)*
LIAM:	It's like the train we saw from Killiney Hill.
SALLY:	Yes. Yes, it is.
GILBERT:	Bravo, Miss Temple – well done.
JOAN:	*(Delighted)* Look – you can see the little things on the wheels and all.
UNA:	And the lights.
GILBERT:	*(Proudly)* Aye – that's OO Gauge.
UNA:	And it's real fast.
JOAN:	*(Interested)* Can you get it to wind in and out around the desks ... ?
GILBERT:	Oh aye – you can change anything. You are in command. In control.
UNA:	*(Watching the train)* Look at the way it wobbles.
DAVE:	*(Suddenly cuddles her)* The way what wobbles?
UNA:	*(Seriously)* Mess off, Dave.
DAVE:	*(Hurt)* 'Mess off', now, is it? For a toy train?
EDDIE:	*(To Miss Temple)* You shouldn't have done that, Miss Temple – repaired the switch-board like that.
MISS TEMPLE:	It's not repaired. I simply connected the railway to the public address socket.
EDDIE:	Well, you shouldn't have done that either.
DAVE:	Right. Let's have the questions.
MISS TEMPLE:	Is it circular, Gilbert?

GILBERT:	Oval-shaped, Miss Temple.
DAVE:	Come on – what about the questions.
GILBERT:	*(Stops the train)* Aye – I'll re-set the lay-out to a different design.
UNA:	*(Disappointed)* Ahhhhh.
JOAN:	*(To Una)* What are you ahhhhing about? He's going to do it again in a different way. *(Sally returns to her desk)*
DAVE:	Are we all in for the questions? Yes? *(Turns out the page)* Mr Donnelly is in. And Eddie? And Joan and Suas-do-guna, Una?
JOAN:	What is it?
DAVE:	Questions.
UNA:	Questions? *(To Joan)* We're not going in for that.
DAVE:	Of course you are. They're easy. Eddie is in.
UNA:	*(To Eddie)* Are you Eddie?
EDDIE:	*(Reluctantly)* Okay fair enough.
DAVE:	Look – here's the first. *(Reads)* 'Who or what were the Oprichniks?' *(Joan and Una giggle)* I'll spell it for you. O-p-r-i-c-h-n-i-k-s. *(Looks up)* Right, who knows? Don't say anything yet. *(Pause)* Una, do you know who the Oprichniks were?
UNA:	*(Pause. Quietly)* No I don't.
DAVE:	I have a good idea myself who they were – but I'm not certain. So, whoever thinks they know, put up their hands. All right? *(Liam, Miss Temple, Christy, Eddie and Dave raise their hands. Then Joan raises her – and tries to get Una to raise hers. Una refuses. Sally continues to work. Gilbert fixes the train)*
DAVE:	You know who they were, do you, Joan?
JOAN:	*(Angrily indicates her raised hand)* Are you blind or something? *(Suddenly realises. To Miss Temple)* Oh Jaysas – sorry.
DAVE:	Sally?
SALLY:	I'm afraid I have to work.
DAVE:	Yeah, handy. *(Pause. Dave threateningly goes from one raised hand to the next)* I won't ask you, Liam. We'll get someone else to give the answer and then each will say whether they think it's right or wrong.

135

	(Pause) Miss Temple. What do you say?
MISS TEMPLE:	*(Hesitates)* Me?
DAVE:	Your hand was up.
CHRISTY:	*(Suddenly)* Yes – you had your hand up.
EDDIE:	*(Aggressively)* That's right – her hand was up.
DAVE:	Yes, your hand was up – what's the answer? Who were the Oprichniks?

MISS TEMPLE: *(Pause)* Well, the Oprichniks were the army of Ivan the Terrible who, on his behalf, disembowelled or boiled alive or dismembered his enemies in great public orgies. *(Silence)* Ivan demanded total allegiance and one day, there was a great gentle elephant brought before him and, because it would not bow to Ivan, the Oprichniks beat it to the ground and then, while it was still alive – they slowly hacked it to pieces with their knives and with their hatchets.

DAVE: *(Quietly)* Jesus Christ.

LIAM: *(Quietly. To Dave)* Is that right, is it?

MISS TEMPLE: *(Quietly)* They started at the elephant's legs ... moved up to his knees and as the blood was now running down along the ...

DAVE: All right! *(Weakly)* Anyone disagree with that?

MISS TEMPLE: It was all on the BBC.

DAVE: Christy?

CHRISTY: *(Puts his head into his hands)* Eh ... eh ... yes, I agree.

EDDIE: *(Weakly)* Yeah, that's it all right. The elephant – I remember reading that, right enough.

DAVE: Yes. I think they were an army formed in 1565 by Ivan the Terrible. We'll see in a minute if we're right. Now ...

UNA: *(To Joan)* Jaysas, I feel awful.

JOAN: What's up with you?

UNA: The elephant. What they done to it.

JOAN: It's only a story. You're as white as a sheet.

CHRISTY: Will I get you some water?

DAVE: *(Concerned)* Put your head between your legs.

JOAN: *(Angrily to Dave)* Will you mess off – can't you see she's sick!

CHRISTY: *(Shaken)* I'll ... I'll get some water.

EDDIE: *(To Christy)* You all right, pal?

CHRISTY:	Of course I'm all right. *(Goes off along corridor)*
UNA:	*(To all)* I ... I'm grand now.
JOAN:	You're like a ghost.
DAVE:	Right. Next one. *(Reads)* Who wrote *The Hunchback of Notre Dame*?
UNA:	*(Weakly)* The Hunchback ... *(Una faints onto the floor)*
JOAN:	Jaysas Una – are you all right?
LIAM:	Is she all right? *(Anxiously to Sally)* Sally?
SALLY:	*(Stands)* Yes?
EDDIE:	Sit her up, sit her up.
LIAM:	*(To Sally)* She fainted ... can you ...?
SALLY:	*(Reluctantly goes over to Una. Now expertly)* Someone open the door – get her some air.
EDDIE:	*(As they sit Una up)* That's it.
LIAM:	She's very pale.
JOAN:	She must've hit her head.
EDDIE:	*(Lightly slaps Una's cheek)* Now, listen to me: What-is-your-name? What-is-your-name?
SALLY:	Do something sensible – open the door ... *(Miss Temple immediately crosses and opens the door)*
EDDIE:	Good idea. *(Jumps up)* She could have concussion, you know. *(Stops. Watches Miss Temple open the door and return to her seat)* My Jaysas!
JOAN:	Has she concussion?
DAVE:	Ah look – her eyes are opening.
JOAN:	Una, love – are you all right?
EDDIE:	*(To Una)* What-is-your-name? Una, what-is-your-name?
SALLY:	*(Annoyed)* Oh, this is silly. Look – we should have her off the floor. We'll put her on that desk there. Liam? Will you ...? *(Indicates carrying Una)*
LIAM:	Oh sure. Dave?
DAVE:	Right. Come on. *(They both lift Una)*
EDDIE:	That's it, lads – between us. *(Stands away. From now, will intently observe Miss Temple)*
LIAM:	*(Carrying Una. To Sally)* Will she be all right, Sally?
SALLY:	Yes, she will – if you don't all crowd around her again. Take her gently. That's fine. *(Una is carefully laid on Dee's desk)*
DAVE:	*(Pause. Seriously)* We should have loosened her

clothes.

JOAN: *(Explodes. To Dave)* Will you mess off, once and for all. It's you and your dirty carry-on that has her this way.

DAVE: Me? What are you talking about?

JOAN: Her fainting! You're old enough to bloody-well know what that means! *(Goes back to Una)*

GILBERT: *(Suddenly anxiously)* The young lady is all right?

MISS TEMPLE: She fainted, Gilbert – when she heard about *The Hunchback of Notre Dame.*

GILBERT: Aye – or the trains, Miss Temple. You can get dizzy watching circular trains.

JOAN: *(To Sally)* Will we give her the kiss of life?

SALLY: *(Annoyed)* Oh, for Heaven's sake! *(Expertly)* Look – raise her feet a little higher. *(Joan reaches for a chair)* No no – here: use these books.*(Una's feet are raised)* That's fine. That's fine now.

EDDIE: *(To Dave, indicates Miss Temple)* Tell me this – how is her lamps?

DAVE: *(Pre-occupied)* Her what?

EDDIE: Did you see her opening the door, fixing the flex – what's the story?

DAVE: *(Pre-occupied)* Oh, her sister reads her books ... and she has a radio ...
(Christy appears along the corridor. He carries water in a milk bottle)

EDDIE: *(To Dave)* Don't cod yourself, pal. What about her singing in the saloon ... *(Sees Christy)* Hey Christy – how bad is your woman's goggles? What's the story?

CHRISTY: She's blind. Can't see. *(Looks around)* Where's Una? *(Goes to Una)* Is she all right?

SALLY: She's all right now. Coming around. *(To Una)* You're all right now. Lie still.

DAVE: *(Anxiously to Liam)* What did Joan mean a minute ago? Did you hear what she said? *(Pause. Annoyed)* When I said about loosening Una's clothes she said it was that kind of thing that had her fainting. *(Pause)* You don't think she could be ...?

LIAM: You mean ...?

DAVE: *(Suddenly)* Jesus, I'll tell you one thing: if she is, it's

138

	not me.
LIAM:	God. *(Pause)* When were you last out with ...?
DAVE:	Me? I wasn't out with her! I saw her only *here* ... and once when ... but that was *nothing*.
EDDIE:	*(Moving away from Miss Temple)* Sitting there ... looking ... like a bleedin' Apache.
DAVE:	*(To Liam)* There must be dozens. And what about all those Arabs in Bahrain? That was only ... how many months ago, was that?
LIAM:	God, it'd be terrible if ...
DAVE:	*(Angrily)* Well, whoever it was, it wasn't me. That, I am certain of. *(Reynolds and Partridge enter from the passageway. Mr Partridge now exudes concern and friendliness)*
LIAM:	*(To Dave)* God – look who's here. *(Dave is pre-occupied)*
EDDIE:	*(Authoritatively)* Ah-ha – just as I expected: the pipe of peace.
PARTRIDGE:	*(Very pleasant)* Good morning. *(Sees Una)* Oh – is someone ill?
SALLY:	I'm afraid she fainted, Mr Partridge.
PARTRIDGE:	*(Affected concern)* Ah – so sorry.
JOAN:	*(Accusingly. Looking towards Dave)* She's been getting sick all the time. Especially in the mornings!
DAVE:	*(Moves)* Jesus. *(Stops)*
PARTRIDGE:	I see. *(Suddenly realises. Shocked)* Oh – I see. Good Heavens. And she's ...? *(Looks at Una's hand)* Is she not married?
JOAN:	*(Aggressively)* No – she's not married.
SALLY:	*(To Una)* Would you like to try sitting? *(Half sits)*
PARTRIDGE:	*(Quietly, furiously to Reynolds)* What the blazes is happening here?
CHRISTY:	*(To Sally, offering the milk bottle)* Here's some water for her.
PARTRIDGE:	*(Suddenly friendly)* Ah, good ... *(Disgusted again)* But that's a dirty milk bottle, eh ... eh ... eh ...
REYNOLDS:	Christy Metcalf, sir.
PARTRIDGE:	*(Friendly)* Ah yes, Christy. And how is your trumpet-playing coming along?
CHRISTY:	*(Coldly)* It's the cornet I play.
PARTRIDGE:	Indeed it is *(Takes the bottle)* Now – I think we can do

	better than this. *(To Reynolds)* Perhaps your Mrs ...?
REYNOLDS:	*(Promptly)* Oh yes, sir – Dee. I'll ask her. *(Walks smartly into his office)*
EDDIE:	*(Quietly to Christy)* This is because Tim Flynn joined our union. Now they *know* they're knackered. *(Sally goes to her desk. Gets some tissues)*
LIAM:	*(Anxiously. To Sally)* Will she be all right?
SALLY:	*(Annoyed. Quietly)* Why are you asking me? I'm not a nurse. *(Goes to Una with tissues)*
PARTRIDGE:	*(Awkward Pause. Now, close to Una)* Tell me, my dear, who is responsible for this? Not a member of my staff, is it? *(He listens. Una whispers. She indicates the office. Dave reacts. Partridge stands erect. Shocked)* What hunchback? *(To Una)* Don't worry, my dear – we'll bring him to heel. *(Partridge, from now, will become noticeably conscious of people's backs. He now notices Christy's while he waits)*
LIAM:	*(To Dave)* They could have changed their minds about me going to the factory.
	(Dee comes from Reynolds' office and hurries off along the corridor)
EDDIE:	*(Now loudly approaching Partridge)* Eh, I suggest, Mr Partridge, that we can adequately attend to this young lady.
PARTRIDGE:	*(Subtly notices Eddie's back)* Of course, Mr ... eh ...?
EDDIE:	Eddie Malone is the name – I'm factory floor shopsteward and the factory-floor representative on the office floor in this current dispute.
PARTRIDGE:	Ah yes, Eddie Malone. Mike tells me that your uncle worked here.
EDDIE:	*(Triumphantly)* He died here, Mr Partridge – on them machines.
PARTRIDGE:	*(Awkwardly)* Yes. Quite. Well. *(Sees Reynolds emerging from his office. Relieved)* Ah – Mike.
REYNOLDS:	Dee – Mrs Kavanagh – is getting something.
PARTRIDGE:	Good *(Confidentially)* A quiet word, Mike. *(They move aside)*
DAVE:	*(Viciously to Liam)* Thinking of it – I'm bloody certain it couldn't have been me. Not in a million years. *(Liam is pre-occupied watching Partridge)* And I don't

	care what anyone says.
PARTRIDGE:	*(Angrily and quietly to Reynolds)* Have we any hunch-backs working here?
REYNOLDS:	*(Pauses thoughtfully)* I beg your pardon, sir.
PARTRIDGE:	*(Furious)* You heard me – hunchbacks. That girl said that a hunchback – *here* – is the cause of ... of her trouble. The staff has gone to blazes without supervision. That's half the trouble – moral collapse. *(Gilbert blows his whistle. The train goes. Furious)* What the ...? *(Recovers)* Gilbert – the ... Duchess of Sutherland, isn't it?
GILBERT:	Aye, Ronnie – just three coaches here – I'll bring in a few viaducts if the strike continues.
	(Dee comes from the corridor with a glass of water, a face towel and some tablets)
PARTRIDGE:	*(Testily, to Gilbert)* Will you now?! *(Sees Dee)* Ah, Mrs Kavanagh ... *(Drinks the water)*
GILBERT:	Aye Ronnie – Albert and Gladys were over last night – had a wonderful lay-out ... talked about London ... and the rusty tattoo needles ...
PARTRIDGE:	*(Quickly)* Ha-ha, old Albert. In good health, is he?
GILBERT:	And good voice. *(Excited)* Remember? *(Sings to the air of 'Twelve Days of Christmas')* Four Marble Arch, Three Bond Street, Two Marlybone and Ronnie ... *(Invites Partridge to finish it)* ... come on, Ronnie ... *(Partridge, throughout this, has been noticing Gilbert's shoulders)*
PARTRIDGE:	Why are your shoulders stooped like that, Gilbert?
GILBERT:	*(Straightens up)* Oh-ho – aye, the old back gets stiff bending over the Chattanooga Cho-Cho *(Sings)* 'Pardon me boy – is that the Chattanooga Cho-Cho?'
PARTRIDGE:	*(Disgusted)* For God's sake, Gilbert!! *(Now business-like)* Mike, perhaps Charlie would like to ...? *(Indicates Christy)*
REYNOLDS:	Of course. *(To Christy)* Christy, Mr Partridge would like a quiet word ...
PARTRIDGE:	*(Pleasantly)* Just an informal little chat. *(To Eddie)* and ... eh ... Neddie, isn't it?
EDDIE:	*(Hard)* It's Eddie! *(Comes over)*
PARTRIDGE:	Of course, Eddie. And the two lads – John and ...?
REYNOLDS:	Dave and Liam.

PARTRIDGE: Dave and Liam. *(Notices their shoulders)* Good – two fine, up-right lads. *(Sits at Liam's desk)* And whose desk is this?

LIAM: Mine, sir.

PARTRIDGE: You won't mind, Liam. *(To Gilbert)* Perhaps Gilbert, you'd turn off that blasted train a moment? *(Studies Gilbert again)*

GILBERT: Oh aye. *(Turns it off)* Albert was saying ...

PARTRIDGE: *(Sharply)* And straighten yourself up. *(Pleasantly to all)* Now, gentlemen – now that we find ourselves with some time on our hands, it may be appropriate to have a little chat about what is happening here – to look at it coolly and simply and to ...

EDDIE: *(Goes to Partridge, followed by Christy. Sharply)* Okay, fair enough, Mr Partridge – we'll look at it coolly and simply: Tim Flynn has joined the union and is, there-fore, party to this stoppage. Nothing moves – belts, ships, nothing.

CHRISTY: *(Confidently. To Reynolds)* And all this ... this softly-softly approach isn't going to cut any ice. We hold the whip-hand now.

REYNOLDS: *(Sharply to Christy)* That's an attitude I wouldn't advise ...

EDDIE: *(Loudly)* Mr Reynolds, things have changed. The glove is on the other foot now. *We* call the shots.

PARTRIDGE: *(Pleasantly)* Of course you do – that's what I say. And that's why I'd like to talk, for a moment about the staff here. The Partridge policy has always been to select staff meticulously. So I know that, in you, I have a good, trustworthy force – oh, we have our grievances – but we have our principles too. *(Pause. With great deliberation)* Gentlemen, I feel that ... that I'm a lucky man, because ...

GILBERT: *(Sings)* 'I'm a lucky boy. You are lucky too.' Eddie?

MISS TEMPLE: *Show Boat*

GILBERT: *Show Boat*. Aye.

PARTRIDGE: *(Furious, but controlled)* I'm a lucky man, because I know that, as morally-conscious people *(Struggles with his feet under the desk)* you have the welfare of this plant at heart. It should be, as I am certain, it is

142

	with all of you ... *(Now reaches down)* ... a priority that not only the conditions of employment ... *(Pulls up Christy's pyjamas. Looks at Liam)* What's this? Yours is it?
LIAM:	No – no, I ...
CHRISTY:	*(Quickly)* It ... It's mine. I must have ... *(Takes the pyjamas)* I must have left it ...
PARTRIDGE:	*(Slowly)* Oh. Yours are they? Here? I see. *(Looks meaningfully from Liam to Christy)*
LIAM:	I didn't know anything about ...
CHRISTY:	It's all right, Liam. *(To Partridge)* I had them here for our ... I'll take them home.
PARTRIDGE:	*(Unable to hide his disgust)* Yes. Do that.
	(Christy will, early in Partridge's next speech, hurriedly throw the pyjamas under Gilbert's desk)
EDDIE:	*(Loudly)* Mr Partridge – that's a red herring. You have come here with no new proposals and ...
PARTRIDGE:	No no, Neddie – hear me out. From our side, we have always tried, staff-wise, to facilitate those ... those unfortunate members of the community who would not otherwise be employable. An example is our *(Quietly)* switchboard operator, Miss Bell.
	(Eddie, particularly, should turn to see Miss Temple tinkering at the switch with a screw-driver and pincers)
REYNOLDS:	*(Corrects Partridge)* Miss Temple.
MISS TEMPLE:	*(Panic. tries to hide the tools)* Yes – calling?
PARTRIDGE:	*(To Miss Temple)* No, my dear – we simply used you as an example ...
EDDIE:	Mr Partridge – we have things to do and you ...
PARTRIDGE:	*(Suddenly angry)* Now just a moment, Neddie ...
EDDIE:	*(Shouts loudly)* Just a moment yourself, Mr Partridge – you have nothing new and we are busy here – we have a strike to run – so, thank you, goodbye and, next time, my name is Eddie. *(Turns)*
CHRISTY:	*(Stands)* Exactly. *(Turns away also)*
PARTRIDGE:	*(Stands. Furiously)* Very well. Then let it be remembered that I came with an olive branch – and you did not even recognise it. *(Turns. Pauses)* And when this is over, there will be a weeding out – a weeding out of not only the inefficient, but of the degenerates who

	have somehow infiltrated my organisation. Good day.
REYNOLDS:	*(Cutting to Christy)* Disputes do end – but what happens during them is seldom forgotten.
CHRISTY:	*(Shouts)* Don't worry – I won't forget. *(Reynolds quickly follows Partridge)*
CHRISTY:	Go on – run after him. *(Loudly)* Lap-dog!
LIAM:	*(Anxiously to Dave)* God – how did those pyjamas get there? *(Dave is pre-occupied)*
EDDIE:	*(Confidently)* There we are, gents – all as anticipated. All par for the course. Next time, they'll have proposals. Right, Dave?
DAVE:	*(Pre-occupied)* What? Oh yeah.
DEE:	*(Comes in angrily from the passageway)* Sally – come on, come on.
CHRISTY:	*(To Dee)* Not much of a big hero now, is he? The great Mike Reynolds – BA, B.Comm.
DEE:	*(Calls out)* Sally! You're not employed here to nurse these people, you know.
SALLY:	*(Suddenly angry)* I wish I wasn't, Mrs Kavanagh! *(Immediate regret)* Sorry – I know I'm not, Mrs Kavanagh. *(Sally sits at her desk. Dee goes off along the corridor with the face towel, water, etc.)*
DAVE:	*(Anxiously to Eddie)* Eddie – is Una often sick?
EDDIE:	Una? Oh yeah – a bit delicate is our Una *(To Christy)* Have you been watching your woman there? *(Indicates Miss Temple)*
CHRISTY:	No. Why?
EDDIE:	Well, I have – and I think she's fixing that switchboard on the sly. *(Miss Temple now sits totally immobile at the switch)*
DAVE:	*(Hopefully to Eddie)* Not very ... strong, is she?
EDDIE:	*(Watching Miss Temple)* Not very strong? She'd knife you in a flash.
CHRISTY:	*(To Eddie)* She seems to be asleep now, Eddie.
DAVE:	*(To Eddie)* Una would knife you?!
EDDIE:	*(Absent)* What? No – Una wouldn't knife anyone. *(To Christy)* She was awake a minute ago.
CHRISTY:	Not a budge out of her now.
DAVE:	*(Mock nonchalance)* No Eddie – I was wondering if

	Una is sick a lot. Is she?
EDDIE:	*(To Christy)* Asleep all right. Ah, that's game-ball so, Christy, we'll leave her.
DAVE:	*(Turns away)* Jesus, why should I worry. It wasn't me and that's that. *(Lighthearted to Liam)* That's the end of it.
	(The telephone rings in Reynolds' office)
SALLY:	*(Unsure. To all)* I'm afraid it's the phone. *(To Liam)* I better go. *(Runs into Reynolds' office. Lifts phone)* Donnycarney Metal Works.
EDDIE:	*(Takes darts from his pocket. Merrily)* Right lads – a game of darts. Dave – you on?
DAVE:	*(Mock good humour)* Darts – oh great idea.
EDDIE:	Christy? Game of darts while things is quiet?
CHRISTY:	Well – I'm not so good. You see, I don't get out much because of the mother.
DAVE:	Come on – you can try. Liam too.
EDDIE:	Now you're talkin'. Anyone else want to play?
MISS TEMPLE:	*(Turns. Enthusiastically)* Yes – I'd like to play. *(Silence)*
EDDIE:	*(Slowly)* What was that, Miss Temple?
MISS TEMPLE:	*(Less enthusiastically)* I'd like to play.
EDDIE:	*(Pause)* You'd like to play what, Miss Temple?
MISS TEMPLE:	*(Softly)* I'd like to play darts.
EDDIE:	You'd like to play darts? *(Looks around)* Right – okay. *(Gives the darts to her)* There you are. You go first. You know where the board is.
SALLY:	*(From Reynolds' office)* Phone call for Eddie Malone.
EDDIE:	Phone call? Blast! *(To Miss Temple)* Don't throw till I get back. *(To Christy)* Tell her.
	(Eddie runs into Reynolds' office. Miss Temple holds the darts)
DAVE:	*(Quietly to Liam)* This should be good.
CHRISTY:	We're not starting yet, Miss Temple. We're going to wait until Eddie has ... *(Suddenly, the conveyor belts clank on and begin to turn. All pause – then panic reaction)*
CHRISTY:	Holy Christ! The belts! The belts are on!
DAVE:	How could ...? What the hell's happening?
CHRISTY:	Eddie? Eddie? *(Goes towards Reynolds' office)*
DEE:	*(Comes delighted from the corridor)* Sally – look! The

	belts are on! *(Sees Christy)* Where are you going? That office is ... *(To stop him)* private!
CHRISTY:	*(Ignores Dee)* Eddie, come out. The Belts are working. *(We see Eddie on the phone. Christy is beside him)*
LIAM:	*(To Sally)* Who was on the phone?
SALLY:	It was a man ...
DEE:	*(Shouts at Sally)* Who allowed those to use that phone? Sally – did you? *(Miss Temple nonchalantly throws the first dart into the floor)*
DAVE:	*(To Liam)* Where's Eddie? Get Eddie – quick!
LIAM:	He's still on the phone. Christy!
DEE:	*(Shouts)* Sally! Answer me – did you?
LIAM:	Christy?
DAVE:	To hell with Christy! *(Goes towards Reynolds' office)* Eddie! *(To Sally)* Who's he on to?
DEE:	*(To all)* This office is private!
DAVE:	*(To Sally)* Who rang him?
SALLY:	*(Screams)* I don't know! *(We see Eddie slam down the phone. He runs out, followed by Christy)*
EDDIE:	*(Furiously)* Where is she? Where is she?
DAVE:	What's happening? Where's who?
EDDIE:	*(To Joan. Slow fury)* There you are! Well congratulations – that's some gobshite of a boyfriend you have in Tim Flynn! Some stupid gobshite he is!
JOAN:	*(Aggressively)* Don't you call him that!
EDDIE:	*(To Joan)* Do you know what he done? Do you?
JOAN:	He joined the union like you told me to tell him.
EDDIE:	*(Shouts to all)* There's only two unions out there – and he's so thick, he went and joined the Drivers and Handlers Union: the one that's *not* on strike! The gobshite joined the only union that's still working – and they, of course, were delighted to get him – delighted to be able to banjo *our* strike. And that's why the belts is on – and that's why we're destroyed!
DAVE:	*(Loudly. To Joan)* There! I knew it! *(To Liam)* That's Tim Flynn for you. *(To Joan)* That's brains, Jesus!
CHRISTY:	What? Then we're ... we're ...?
EDDIE:	We're bleedin' destroyed, pal. We might as well go back *now!*

146

DEE:	*(To Christy)* Ha! Now. Now look at the great hero!
	(Miss Temple nonchalantly throws the second dart. This lands close to Christy. He sees it)
EDDIE:	Just as we were winning, the gobshite has us back working again!
CHRISTY:	*(Furiously)* Well, that switchboard isn't going to be working. *(Moves quickly towards the switch)*
LIAM:	*(Anxiously)* No – Christy, don't!
	(Christy collides with Miss Temple as she holds up the third dart. He cries out. Stops. Holds his face)
CHRISTY:	What was ... that? *(He turns. He is bleeding heavily)* Oh mother. I'm bleeding.
EDDIE:	Jesus Christ, Christy – your face!
LIAM:	Sally! Quick!
CHRISTY:	I'm cut to bits! Look. Oh mother.
SALLY:	*(Runs over. Angrily to Liam)* Why *me*? *(She now tries to get Christy into a chair)*
DEE:	What the hell is happening here?
CHRISTY:	*(Panic)* Look – blood!
JOAN:	Jaysas, his face – it's gushing out!
SALLY:	Leave him! Don't crowd around!
CHRISTY:	Oh mother! My face!
DAVE:	What happened to him?
LIAM:	Oh, my God!
EDDIE:	*(Looks at the wound)* You're right, pal – it's slashed right through.
SALLY:	*(Angrily to Eddie)* Don't say that! *(To Christy)* Mr Metcalf – we'll just open your collar.
DEE:	*(Angrily)* Sally – come here. Do you think this is a bloody hospital?
LIAM:	*(To Dee)* Christy ran right into the dart that Miss Temple had.
EDDIE:	*(Loudly)* Ran into it?! *(Wild irony)* She got him! I said this'd happen. First, Black Eagle; now, Christy Metcalf. The question is – who's next on her list?
	(Una faints. Joan goes to her. Miss Temple stands away)

BLACK OUT
END OF SCENE ONE, ACT TWO

ACT TWO

Scene Two

An hour later. The belts are working. Miss Temple helps Gilbert to dismantle his train. Sally is at her desk. Liam is beside Sally. Dee is in Reynolds' office. Dave moves nervously about.

LIAM: *(Defensively to Sally)* I only asked you if he'd be all right ... *(Pause)* ... because you attended to him. *(Sally looks up angrily)* Well, you did.

EDDIE: *(Arriving up from the factory floor, now shouts down)* Tell Billy, I'll be down in a minute. *(Pause)* No – I've seen no one yet. *(Enters the office)*

DEE: *(Comes briskly out)* Sally, after that, get me the Hamburg contract from the files room. *(To Liam)* I think your desk is over there. *(Returns to the office)*

SALLY: *(To Liam)* You better go.

LIAM: *(As he goes)* I'll be going everywhere soon. *(Angrily)* Probably be down there on the factory floor tomorrow – calling off machine numbers.

MISS TEMPLE: I'll wind this flex for you Gilbert.

GILBERT: Oh, many thanks, Miss Temple.

EDDIE: *(To Dave)* Opening doors, directing people, throwing darts, now winding flex. That's blind, is it?

DAVE: *(Pause)* Eh, meant to ask you, Eddie – has Una a big family?

EDDIE: *(Absently, watching Miss Temple)* Una? Oh, I think she's down in the ladies. With Joan. *(Of Miss Temple)* Look at her now.

LIAM: *(To Dave)* Poor Christy looked ashen being carried out, didn't he?

DAVE: *(To Liam)* Yeah, he did. *(To Eddie)* No, I said has Una big family? *(Silence)* Has she any brothers?

EDDIE: *(Pause. Looks at Miss Temple)* Bleedin' Apaches. *(Partridge and Reynolds come quickly along the passageway)*

PARTRIDGE: *(Smartly, to Reynolds)* How much time, Mike?

REYNOLDS: *(Checks his watch)* Five minutes, sir.

PARTRIDGE: Good. *(To all. Sharply)* A moment, everybody. *(Sits at Gilbert's desk)*

REYNOLDS: *(To Partridge)* Excuse me, sir. *(To Eddie)* Mr Malone, please? *(Indicates his office)* You may wait in my office, if you wish.

EDDIE: What? *(Realises)* Oh, quite understand. Indubiously. Yes. *(Goes into Reynolds' office)*

PARTRIDGE: Oh. Well done, Mike. *(Sits at Gilbert's desk. To all)* Now, we are, as you know, at the end of a disgraceful and distasteful occurrance. On an industrial level, I am glad to see that the factory has resumed work and the clerical staff will resume normal duties as soon as possible. On a personal level, however, I have despaired of you – a staff that I felt was hand-picked for their good character – yet a staff that indulged in ... what? – factory girls frolicking through the offices, a stabbing on the premises, a blind woman assaulted, *(Struggles with his feet under the desk)* a young girl claiming she was impregnated by a hunchback, a switchboard destroyed, a man's pyjamas found under the desk of a junior clerk *(Reaches down)* ... what the blazes ... *(Pulls up Christy's pyjamas)* ... and now, another pyjamas! Who owns this one?

LIAM: *(Immediately)* No ... it's ... that is the ...

PARTRIDGE: *(Disgusted. To Liam)* Oh – your one, is it?

LIAM: *(Upset)* No – it's the one that was ...

PARTRIDGE: *(To all)* This is what I'm talking about. *(Throws the pyjamas to Liam)* Put that with Charlie's and take the two of them out of here. *(To all)* And let's hope that we've seen the last of this disgusting behaviour and that Donnycarney Metal Works will, once again, be a factory to be proud of. *(Pause)* Now – to business, Mike.

REYNOLDS: Thank you, sir. Christy Metcalf will be unfit for duty for some time. Management, therefore, has decided to fill his position immediately promoting a member of *(looks around at all)* this staff. The appointment will be an interim one – but with the possibility of permanency. Mr Metcalf's position will, therefore, be

	filled by ... David McKeever.
DAVE:	*(Amazed. Delighted)* Who me? Me?
REYNOLDS:	*(Smartly)* Yes. Congratulations. Welcome to the team.
PARTRIDGE:	*(Notices his back)* It's a step up, you'll be on trial – but I hear you're a good lad and we shall see. *(Pointedly)* Any questions?
DAVE:	Questions? No sir. Thank you, sir.
PARTRIDGE:	Anything on your mind? Anxieties?
	(Joan and Una come along the corridor. Una is very weak)
DAVE:	No – none sir. And thanks very much, sir. *(Sees Una. Quietly)* Oh, good Jesus!
PARTRIDGE:	Ah, how are we, ladies?
JOAN:	*(Grumpily)* Be glad to get back to the factory – away from all the messin' up in this place.
UNA:	Hello Dave. *(He looks away. She is hurt)*
PARTRIDGE:	Yes – well, before you resume your duties ... Mike, you can get that Neddie fellow out now.
REYNOLDS:	*(Calls)* Mr Malone! *(Eddie comes quietly out)* With regard to the factory, it has been decided that new safety regulations will be introduced across the factory floor ... *(Offers Eddie the official proposal letter)*
PARTRIDGE:	*(To Eddie)* ... because of what happened to your uncle – falling into the machines ...
EDDIE:	*(Puzzled)* The what? *(Thinks quickly – now suddenly delighted)* Oh that's ... eh ... yes, that is ... *(Takes the proposal letter from Reynolds. Now with great confidence)* That is, *inter alia*, a very satisfactory outcome to our long-standing grievances re safety measures ...
MISS TEMPLE:	But I thought your uncle died of a heart attack, Mr Malone.
EDDIE:	*(Pause)* Excuse me. Mr Partridge. *(Goes to Miss Temple. Controlled)* No, lady – the poor uncle fell into the machines. All right?
JOAN:	*(To Una)* Oh, put your hands over your ears, Una. *(Una does this)*
MISS TEMPLE:	So you're saying now that he did, in fact, die piece by piece?
EDDIE:	*(Furiously)* All right all right! Have it your way: my uncle Barney was cut up in bits, gushing blood – just ... just like your bleedin' elephant. Now are you sat-

isfied?

PARTRIDGE: *(Aghast)* Elephant? What's this about an elephant?

EDDIE: *(Nonchalantly to Partridge)* Ah this was an elephant that they chopped up with hatchets because it would not do what it was told.

JOAN: *(To Una)* Not yet. *(Una keeps her hands over her ears)*

PARTRIDGE: *(Aghast)* Here? This happened here?

DAVE: No, sir – in Russia. The Oprichniks owned it.

EDDIE: *(To Partridge)* It was in the paper this morning.

PARTRIDGE: *(Relaxes)* Ah, I see – in Russia? *(Authoritatively)* Well, I think that should be a lesson to all of you – and you should be grateful that you're negotiating with Partridges in Ireland and not with those Oprichniks in Russia.

EDDIE: *(Relaxes)* Oh, indubiously, indubiously. *(Indicates the proposal letter. Gratefully)* And I feel, sir, the members will be delighted with these proposals.

JOAN: *(To Una)* It's all right now. *(Una takes her hands away from her ears and relaxes)*

PARTRIDGE: Good. Well now I suggest we all resume normal duties. *(To Una)* And don't worry, my dear – we'll soon trace that hunchback. *(Goes, with Reynolds, into Reynolds' office*

Una immediately faints. Joan tries to lift her)

EDDIE: *(Runs to Una)* Ah, she's gone again. *(To Joan)* Come on, both of us can ...

JOAN: *(Angrily to Eddie)* Leave her alone. I can manage. Gobshite.

EDDIE: Now wait a minute, Joan – we have succeeded in implementing safety regulations across the factory floor ...

(Una, ignored, begins to crawl to the door. Miss Temple walks across and opens the door)

JOAN: *(To Eddie)* This strike wasn't about safety regulations ...

EDDIE: Joan, it was always a consideration of our union that ...

JOAN: Consideration! What would you know about consideration?

EDDIE: No Joan – our primary concern in industrial action ...

JOAN: ... and then you talk about Tim Flynn? You're the gobshite! *(Now sees Una)* Ah Una. *(Helps her out*

151

	through the door)
EDDIE:	*(Very angry)* Look here, Joan – these safety regulations were granted because my uncle Barney fell into the machines and ...
MISS TEMPLE:	*(To Eddie)* Then, Mr Malone, you're quite adamant that he didn't die of a heart attack?
EDDIE:	*(Furiously to Miss Temple)* Don't start on me again, lady – or I'll say something that you'll regret.
JOAN:	*(Off)* Gobshite! *(Eddie reacts)*
MISS TEMPLE:	*(Calmly)* Mr Malone – I'm simply wondering how you managed to get safety regulations when ... *(Partridge re-enters from Reynolds' office)*
EDDIE:	*(Loudly and viciously)* All right! I'll tell you how I managed it. I managed it the same way as you managed to go through every saloon in Canada, singing songs and knifing people – and then, when it suited you, to change your name to Miss Temple, come over here and say the only thing you're good at is working telephones. I managed it the same as that. Okay?
MISS TEMPLE:	*(Calmly)* Oh, fair enough, Mr Malone.
EDDIE:	*(Furiously)* And fair enough yourself, Miss Temple ... *(Viciously, directed towards Partridge)* ... or should I say – Rose Marie! *(Shocked silence. Partridge watches Eddie depart; watches Miss Temple return to her seat)*
DEE:	*(Comes from Reynolds' office. Very breezy)* Sally, did you get that Hamburg contract?
SALLY:	*(Recovers)* What? Oh –I'll get it now, Mrs Kavanagh. *(Hurries off along the corridor)*
DEE:	*(Brightly)* Coffee, Mr Partridge? *(Reynolds re-enters)* Mike?
PARTRIDGE:	*(Recovers)* Eh, no, thank you – we're having some dinner now – and perhaps David would like to come along? *(To Dave)* Like to have a little chat with you.
DAVE:	*(Delighted)* Oh – thank you very much, sir.
PARTRIDGE:	Good then.
REYNOLDS:	*(To Liam)* You – you be in my office at nine o'clock sharp tomorrow and I'll give you your new duty roster in some detail!
LIAM:	*(Realises. Downcast)* What? *(Looks at the machines)* Oh

yes –

PARTRIDGE: *(Furiously to Liam)* And will you kindly take all those degenerate pyjamas off these premises now!

LIAM: What? Oh yes, sir. *(Goes off quickly, trailing the pyjamas)*

PARTRIDGE: *(Pause, now relieved)* Right – I think that's everything, Mike. *(Cutting)* We'll leave Gilbert here – playing with his little train. *(General laughter from Dee, Reynolds, Dave and Partridge)*

GILBERT: *(Slightly embarrassed)* Will I tell Albert that ...

REYNOLDS: *(To Partridge)* And wearing his hat.

PARTRIDGE: *(Appreciates this)* Indeed, Mike. *(To Gilbert)* Or you can be singing, Gilbert – you can be singing one of your silly little songs. *(Laughter again – while Dave whispers to Reynolds)*

GILBERT: *(Very embarrassed)* Ronnie, will I tell Albert and Gladys that you might come over and ...

PARTRIDGE: *(To Dee)* Good-day to you now, Mrs ... eh ... must get back to normal.

DEE: *(Having taken a large bunch of flowers from a vase to re-arrange. Sweetly)* Yes – good-day to you, Mr Partridge.

REYNOLDS: *(To Partridge)* Did you hear, sir – Dave calls him 'The Singing Hat'.

PARTRIDGE: *(Delighted)* Ha-ha-, excellent. Indeed he is 'The Singing Hat' – if you ever heard a hat singing to a toy train! *(General laughter and they are gone)*

GILBERT: *(Pause. Quietly sings. Hurt. As he packs his train)* Grab your hat and get your coat, leave your worries on the doorstep ...

(The phone rings in Reynolds' office. Dee, still holding the flowers, runs to answer it)

MISS TEMPLE: *(Gently)* It is a pity that we didn't have time for the full lay-out, Gilbert – for the viaducts.

GILBERT: *(Still packing the train)* Aye, Miss Temple – it is.

MISS TEMPLE: *(Gently)* That would have been nice.

GILBERT: That would have been very nice.

MISS TEMPLE: Yes. You would have enjoyed that. *(Gilbert carries the carton to his desk. Miss Temple puts her tools away)*

GILBERT: Aye, I would – but our golden days were short, Miss Temple.

MISS TEMPLE: Indeed they were, Gilbert.

GILBERT: *(Sings)* Golden days in the sunshine of our happy youth; golden days full of innocence ...

(Suddenly the belts stop. There is a deadly silence. Gilbert stands – then runs over to look down at the factory. Miss Temple is immobile)

DEE: *(Angrily into phone)* What the hell are you talking about? *(Pause)* Who has gone on strike? The Drivers and Handlers Union? *(Pause)* Hold on! *(Runs angrily out into the office, still carrying her flowers. Sees the silent factory)* Oh shit! *(Sees Gilbert. Angrily)* You! What are you doing standing there? *(Viciously indicates the factory with the bunch of flowers)* Get Ronnie Partridge back up here, quick! *(Runs back into Reynolds' office, leaving Gilbert oscillating between confusion and delight)*

MISS TEMPLE: Oh Gilbert, if they are ...

GILBERT: *(Listening)* Shhhhhhhhh.

DEE: *(Angrily. Into phone)* Hello – isn't that the union that sod Tim what's-his-name joined? *(Pause)* Oh shit!

GILBERT: *(Delighted. To Miss Temple)* You're right, my dear.

(Gilbert now replaces the carton on the floor and begins to enthusiastically unpack the train and track. Miss Temple excitedly takes out her tools to connect the plugs)

MISS TEMPLE: *(Excited)* Oh good.

DEE: *(Angrily into phone)* Ah what do you mean the Handlers want parity with the beltman's working hours?

MISS TEMPLE: *(To Gilbert)* Gilbert, now you can bring in all your French trains and all your cross-overs and all your marshalling yards ...

GILBERT: *(Excited. Setting up the railway)* I certainly can, Miss Temple.

DEE: *(Angrily into phone)* Yes yes yes – we're trying to get Mr Partridge now.

MISS TEMPLE: *(Excited)* And the viaducts, Gilbert – will you be able to bring in your viaducts?

GILBERT: Indeed I will. *(Sings merrily)* Four viaducts, three French trains, two turtle doves – and Ronnie Partridge ... *(To Miss Temple)* Come on, my dear – where is he?

MISS TEMPLE: *(Excited)* Look, Gilbert. *(Indicates the PA microphone)* I think I may have this working now.

GILBERT: Oh lovely. Perfect. *(Clears his throat)*

(Dee rushes out from Reynolds' office. She still carries the flowers – now somewhat broken. She stops. Horrified to see Gilbert with Miss Temple)

DEE: *(Furiously)* Mr Donnelly! *(Controlled)* Mr Donnelly, I thought I told you to find Ronnie Partridge for me? *(Slight pause. Furiously)* So where is he?

GILBERT: *(Confused)* Aye – so where is he? *(Suddenly relaxes. Joking to Miss Temple)* So where is he, Miss Temple?

MISS TEMPLE: *(Almost giggles)* Where is he?

GILBERT/MISS TEMPLE: *(Towards Dee, singing slowly, with great feeling, into the microphone – their voices booming over the factory)* Ronnie Partridge is up a pear tree!

DEE: *(Furiously, as they finish)* Oh, for God's sake!

(Angrily flings the flowers at them, storms back into Reynolds' office and slams the door. Gilbert is seen to regard the thrown flowers as an appreciation bouquet, picks up one flower, presents it to Miss Temple – as we immediately fade to blackout)

THE END

NOTES

156

NOTES

NOTES

NOTES

NOTES